PREPARED

PREPARED

A MANUAL FOR SURVIVING
WORST-CASE SCENARIOS

MIKE GLOVER

Portfolio | Penguin

Portfolio / Penguin
An imprint of Penguin Random House LLC
penguinrandomhouse.com

Most Portfolio books are available at a discount when purchased in quantity
for sales promotions or corporate use. Special editions, which include personalized
covers, excerpts, and corporate imprints, can be created when purchased in large
quantities. For more information, please call (212) 572-2232 or e-mail
specialmarkets@penguinrandomhouse.com. Your local bookstore
can also assist with discounted bulk purchases using the Penguin Random
House corporate Business-to-Business program. For assistance in locating
a participating retailer, e-mail B2B@penguinrandomhouse.com.

Library of Congress record available at https://lccn.loc.gov/2022052025

ISBN 9780593538142 (hardcover)
ISBN 9780593538159 (ebook)

Printed in the United States of America
3rd Printing

BOOK DESIGN BY CHRIS WELCH

For my son Benjamin and my daughter Penelope,

in hopes that your dad gave you all the

tools needed to thrive.

CONTENTS

FOREWORD

By Jack Carr

n the Melian Dialogue of his *History of the Peloponnesian War*, the Athenian historian Thucydides characterizes *hope* as *danger's comforter*. In modern military and intelligence parlance, the ancient Greek general's text translates as *hope is not a course of action*. The lesson is one as old as time: be prepared.

For most of human history, one didn't have a choice. One had to be prepared to survive. Your life and the lives of your family and tribe, the very preservation of society, depended on it. You also had to be good at two things: fighting and hunting.

Hunting and war are inexorably mixed. They share a common father. Death begets life and killing is often a part of the equation. Throughout most of human history, defeating an enemy in battle led to the survival of the tribe and the continuation of the bloodline. The tools developed to defeat rivals in combat are analogous to those used in the quest for sustenance.

Similar tactics are used to hunt both man and beast. Those who picked up a spear to defend the tribe were the same ones who used that spear to provide food for their families. In fact, the reason each and every one of us is alive today is the martial prowess and hunting abilities of our ancestors. The tools have evolved but the reasons to be proficient in their use have not.

John Steinbeck wrote in *The Acts of King Arthur and His Noble Knights*: "I will lay down the law and you will learn it word by word, and every word must be edged with fire. This is the law. The purpose of fighting is to win. There is no possible victory in defense. The sword is more important than the shield, and skill is more important than either. The final weapon is the brain, all else is supplemental."

Modern life, particularly in the West, is marked by comfort and a detachment from what Jack London called "the law of club and fang" unknown in the annals of human history. Today, it is possible to stumble through life with blinders on, shielded from the harsher realities that were inescapable just a century ago. Grocery stores are never empty of food, gas stations are always open and have fuel available, air-conditioning and heating units insulate us from the environment, mechanics keep your car running, electricians and plumbers can be called to maintain your home, banks safeguard your money. In the Western world, life can run fairly smoothly. That is, until calamity strikes.

That calamity may appear in the form of a natural disaster, a medical emergency, or a violent crime. Modern societal impulses encourage us to call 9-1-1 in the event of an emergency. Someone will be there to answer the call and send police officers, firefighters, or EMTs to the rescue. Or will they? Will those first responders be there in time to fend off an assault, put out a fire, or apply a tourniquet? Or will they arrive after the event to take reports and clean up the mess? As the saying goes, "The police are minutes away when seconds count."

Whose responsibility is it to protect you and your loved ones? Whose responsibility is it to be ready? Unless you are a politician with taxpayer-funded 24/7 security, I can tell you the answer: it is ours. As citizens, we have responsibilities that extend beyond paying taxes. We have a responsibility to our families, our communities, and our country to be assets, not liabilities. That means we need to train.

My friend Mike Glover, former U.S. Army Special Forces soldier and CIA contractor, lives in the preparedness space. As the founder of Fieldcraft Survival, his mission is to educate, train, and equip citizens to deal with worst-case scenarios. But mere survival is not the goal. The goal is to prevail. That means recognizing the need to be prepared and then doing what is necessary to get there. That you are holding this book tells me you are taking steps toward becoming an asset.

In the pages that follow, Mike provides the groundwork for what it means to be a prepared citizen. Take it to heart and use it as a foundation upon which to build. It is not enough to have a fire extinguisher, a trauma kit, and a firearm. We must know how to use them. Wise words from Archilochus, c. 650 BC, remind us that "we don't rise to the level of our expectations, we fall to the level of our training." Mike and his cadre at Fieldcraft Survival are there to ensure that your level of training is second to none, that when the time comes to save the most precious of gifts, that of life, you are ready.

Will there come a day when your survival or your family's survival depends on primordial abilities? Will you be relying on hope, mercy from those who would do you harm, or government intervention to save you? Will you rely on luck to pull you through? A commanding officer in the SEAL Teams once told me: "Luck is the residue of preparation." That preparation starts now. Turn the page. Be an asset. Your future and the future of the nation depend on it.

—Jack Carr is a former Navy SEAL sniper, host of the *Danger Close* podcast, and the #1 *New York Times* bestselling author of the James Reece *Terminal List* series.

PREPARED

INTRODUCTION

Catastrophe. What feelings does that word conjure up for you?

If you're like most people, catastrophe typically takes the nightmarish form of a cataclysmic, world-altering natural disaster: a meteor strike, a volcanic eruption, an avalanche, a tsunami flood, an 8-magnitude earthquake, a Category 5 hurricane, a typhoon, an F5 tornado. While these are certainly examples of catastrophic events, they don't even come close to completing the catalog of possible catastrophes one might experience, because it doesn't take the entire world being ripped apart for something to ruin your life or jeopardize your health. The impact doesn't have to extend beyond the world of a small family or a single person for an unexpected, violent, out-of-control event to qualify as a catastrophe for *you*.

This book is a set of preparedness-first principles designed to

help you survive *any* kind of catastrophe in the modern world.*
When I talk about catastrophe, it is this more expansive definition of the term that I'm using. It includes natural disasters, of
course, but also man-made disasters like an active shooter, nuclear accident, civil unrest, power grid collapse, structure fire,
home invasion, car accident, hiking accident, carjacking, and
any other event that is out of your control where your physical
safety is threatened, and death or grievous bodily harm are a
real possibility.

The principles of modern preparedness are divided roughly
into two parts: the mental versus the physical, the internal versus the external, the intangible versus the tangible.

A resilient mindset, proper planning, situational awareness,
and good decision-making compose the first half of these principles. This is the mental, intangible side of preparedness. It's
the piece you can't buy, that you can't hold in your hands.
It's the piece you have to build. These four elements are about
getting and keeping your head in the game if and when things
go bad.

The second half includes principles regarding everyday carry

---

*What this book does *not* include are principles related strictly to primitive
survival. You are not going to read about rubbing sticks together to create fire,
or capturing water in an underground still, or learning which wild mush-
rooms and berries are safe to eat. Those topics are the purview of primitive
survivalists, and while they are very interesting and incredibly useful if you
find yourself stranded in the wilderness for a long time, they are not as helpful
for the kind of modern preparedness we are going to talk about in this book.

(EDC), mobility, and the homestead. These are tangible tools and assets that you can imagine as a set of concentric circles of physical preparedness. They constitute the things you will need on your person, in your vehicle, and around your home to be confident that you won't just survive a catastrophe but will thrive in it.

Combined, these seven principles form a matrix of preparedness that, when embraced and trained and kept sharp, creates the most potent kind of self-reliance. The kind that reduces anxiety and daily low-grade stress while simultaneously setting you up to handle the sudden periods of high-grade stress that are the hallmark of catastrophe in all its forms.

SADR CITY

I came to understand the power of mental preparedness during my twenty-year career as a US Army Green Beret and CIA contractor. Across fifteen deployments and combat rotations to numerous countries, from Iraq and Afghanistan to Libya and Yemen, I witnessed or personally confronted every kind of catastrophic event you would expect a multitour combat veteran might face. In my quest to survive these encounters and to succeed in my various roles, I also found many of the tools of preparedness that reliably increased my chances of survival and success. But it was in Sadr City, Iraq, in 2006, as a sergeant on a mission that nearly killed me, where I saw how these two sides of preparedness actually come together.

The mission itself was unique for a couple reasons. One, it was not a standard direct-action mission* like we were used to as a special operations unit; instead, it was a hostage-rescue mission in a building right on the edge of the city. Two, instead of being conducted lightning fast with overwhelming force, and relying on small, agile teams and the element of surprise, the mission involved an armor and mechanized infantry unit of the regular army.† There is nothing small or agile about that.

My role on this mission was to link up with a column of tanks and Bradley fighting vehicles and lead the security team in my sector, as part of the outer cordon of the battle space. Our job was to provide supporting fire to the team breaching the target building and to repel enemy elements attempting to join the fight from outside the city. And there were likely to be a lot of enemy elements. This was the height of Muqtada al-Sadr's power in Iraq. His Mahdi Army was wreaking havoc in Baghdad—the Sadr City district in particular—as part of the Sunni-Shia sectarian conflict that had caught fire after na-

---

*"Direct-action" is a term used in the military to refer to raids, attacks, ambushes, or assaults that are typically short in duration and conducted by small special operations units to seize, destroy, kill, capture, exploit, or recover designated targets.

†In the US Army, an armor and mechanized infantry company includes tanks and armored personnel carriers. These are big and loud and conspicuous—basically the exact opposite of how special operations units train to fight.

tional elections in early 2005. Even though we moved in quietly under the cover of darkness, once they heard from their network of early informers where we were, they'd be coming.

Sure enough, when our guys breached the door of the target building, the fighting kicked off almost immediately. We started to receive fire from inside the target building and from adjacent structures, and we were getting reports that enemy combatants—on foot and in vehicles—were trying to make their way toward us, both from adjacent neighborhoods inside the city and from the fields just beyond the city limits behind us. Very quickly, I realized that from our position we couldn't see shit. The tanks and Bradleys had powerful, remote weapons systems and mounted large-caliber guns that made them deadly effective, but we only had a single line of sight toward the target building. We were completely blind in every other direction. That was, to put it lightly, not good.

I immediately identified a three-story building offset from the target that offered a 360-degree view of the battle space. I grabbed a couple machine gun teams from the regular army unit to breach the front door, and we quickly made our way to the roof to set up what was basically an overwatch position, with gunners on every corner of the building.

That's how we finally got the full picture of what we were dealing with, both incoming and outgoing.

Right away, a young private who was covering the fields on the outskirts of town called to me, unsure of what to do. "Hey, Sergeant! There are two figures headed this direction!"

"Are they armed?" I asked.

"I'm not sure, I think so."

"Then what are you waiting for? Light them up," I yelled.

It was a typical command in the heat of combat, but I issued it more urgently and angrily than usual because I was struggling to do that very thing from my position facing the target building. None of my shots were having any effect on the enemy. We were too far away. When we spun up from base earlier that night, I'd lined out my kit with an M-4 as my primary weapon, outfitted with a 10.5-inch barrel. That would be perfectly effective for ground fighting and close quarters battle, which is what I expected to be doing as part of the mechanized column that made up the outer cordon. From a three-story rooftop, it simply wasn't enough.

Eventually, the growing enemy force got a bead on where we were firing from, and we started to receive incoming small-arms fire, machine-gun fire, and rocket-propelled grenade (RPG) rounds, which kept us on the rooftop longer than we wanted. The increase in fighting also started to extend the mission for much longer than had been initially planned. We were creeping up on daylight, and daylight is something we try to avoid at all costs in Special Operations because we lose some of our technical and tactical advantage. We also run the risk of losing our close air support from the Little Bird and Black Hawk helicopters, because they become much easier to shoot down.

Fortunately, we had an F-16 from the navy as part of our close air support package that could stay on target longer.

Unfortunately, communications got crossed up with the F-16 pilot as we moved into daybreak, so when he saw gunfire coming from our rooftop position, he assumed we were enemy combatants. I only know this for a fact in retrospect, but I could sense it in the moment when I saw the F-16 break out of its normal patrol pattern and start to loop around. I'd seen navy jets do this countless times before when they were initiating a gun run or an ordnance drop. This guy was about to dust us. And every single one of us on the rooftop saw him coming.

In a moment like this, you do not have time to think. An F-16 can reach Mach 2, or twice the speed of sound. Once it's vectored in on your position, with its straight-line speed you have seconds—to react, not to think. When I saw the jet come around and begin its run, I ripped into my kit and pulled out a VS17 panel and laid it out in the middle of the rooftop. A VS17 panel is a highly reflective fluorescent orange-and-pink cloth panel that is used in the military to identify friendly forces. I've packed this piece of cloth, almost unconsciously, as a matter of muscle memory, in the same spot in my kit for nearly every mission in my twenty years of service. I can count on one hand the number of times I've needed to use it. This was the first. Thank God the pilot saw it.

Back at base, after the unexpectedly long but successful mission, many of my teammates found me and checked in. *Dude. What the fuck, man. That was close. You good?* I told them I was, even if, in the moment, I wasn't sure. As a brotherhood, they knew it was possible to get deep in your head after a close call like that. They knew I needed a distraction. They wanted me to know that I wasn't alone and that I had support all around me. They wanted me to know that they knew that I'd nearly just taken a big bite of a huge shit sandwich.

IT'S ALL ABOUT PREPAREDNESS

We like to think about combat and catastrophe as distinct ideas, as different things. But qualitatively, they're the same.

A malevolent force that is trying to kill you? Check.

Surround-sound chaos and uncertainty everywhere you turn? Check.

Sudden, violent, terrifying incidents that can create lasting trauma? Check.

Acts of God or acts of madness that defy explanation? Check.

The only difference between combat and catastrophe is that combat is a choice, while catastrophe is something that happens *to* you or *around* you. Regardless, the only things that can equip you to respond to either, that can insulate you from the fatal consequences of either, that can set you up to thrive in *and* after either . . . are the pillars of preparedness.

The resilience I developed during my previous combat deployments allowed me to keep my cool on that rooftop in Sadr City while enemy rounds zipped overhead and the American F-16 started to bear down on us. I had a moment there when I said to myself, "Jesus, Mike, you're gonna fucking die up here." But it was just a moment. If it had been any longer, it could have shut me down. Instead, I told myself out loud, "Stop it, Mike. No. You're not going to die." And when I said that, I was able to get right back to work.

The planning we did in the days prior to this specific mission, and the planning we bake into each discrete aspect of a combat mission, gave us the confidence that we knew what to do, and then what to do when that first thing didn't work out. If the team breaching the door of the target building failed, we had contingencies for that. If one of us got wounded, we know that the treatment plan was a three-step progression: self-aid, buddy aid, then corpsman aid. There was never any question, in any phase of the mission, of what to do next.

The situational awareness I developed over years of training, of combat patrols, and of vigilance back stateside kept my head on a swivel from the moment we left base. It's what allowed me to recognize so quickly that we were in a disadvantageous position on the ground, that there was a building nearby that could rectify the problem, and that we were in trouble with that F-16.

The decision-making ability I cultivated as an operator (who was expected to solve many of his own problems) and then honed as a team leader (who was expected to also be able to help others solve their problems) was what made my decisions to move to the rooftop and then to deploy the VS-17 panel, instantaneous.

The rigor and deliberateness of everyday carry considerations is what ensured that the VS-17 panel was in my pack in the first place.

The increased capacity and flexibility of our vehicular support (armored personnel carriers, Humvees, tanks, helicopters) made exfiltration from the battle zone, despite extending into daylight, not just possible but effective.

The built-out security and resourcing at our base made it possible to be fully provisioned outside the wire and made it safe for us to return and recuperate and debrief so that we could succeed at an even higher level the next time we went out on a mission.

In catastrophe, you can derive the same kinds of benefits from sufficient preparedness that we get from them in combat. When you remove the tactical military layer from preparedness and strip it down to its foundational elements, it becomes clear as day that an integrated sense of preparedness can help any person out there prevent, survive, and overcome any kind of disaster they might face.

In this book, I'm going to show you how.

THE RESILIENT MINDSET

Catastrophe is an equal opportunist. It doesn't care about your personal wealth or social status, your religious convictions, or how nice of a person you are. Catastrophe doesn't operate or execute on timelines and constraints. It doesn't have an objective or a goal outside of turning your life into complete and utter chaos. The question here is, are you prepared? Are you ready to be confronted—head-on—by the worst day of your life?

In preparedness, it is often said, mindset is everything. You hear that phrase a lot from those who have built a business around the idea of "improving your mindset." What I've often found is that the so-called experts don't have any tangible advice for improving mindset. Like, how do I actually make my mindset better, and what is mindset in the first place? Let's start off by answering those basic questions.

Many people walk through life either numb or vibrating from self-induced anxiety. They have lots of everyday worries that have fried their brains and maxed their capacity to cope with life's curveballs. This has become the new baseline in modern society. We have grown accustomed to lives full of low-grade stress that cause us to overreact emotionally. This means we underrespond cognitively and fail to source solutions that lead to improved outcomes. This ultimately leads to disastrous results when we are confronted with compressed timelines and high-grade stress, otherwise known as catastrophe. Essentially, we have redefined our baseline coping mechanisms and are less resilient as a society.

When I talk about having the right mindset, what I'm referring to is resilience—having the ability to withstand the initial shock when catastrophe strikes, and then having the wherewithal to respond in a timely and constructive manner. A resilient mindset is *everything*, because your ability to withstand an acutely traumatic event and respond to it may very well mean the difference between life and death.

It doesn't get more conclusive than that.

Of course, it's not so simple as knowing what to say or what to do and then wishing resilience into existence. To develop resilience requires training and exposure. It requires an understanding of stress and how both the mind and body respond to it. And to understand *that*, you first and foremost require a solid grasp on your very own mental machinery.

THE NERVOUS SYSTEM

The brain is the command center of the body. Nearly every action the body takes, whether it's voluntary (like walking and talking) or involuntary (like breathing and blinking), is initiated in the brain. The signal runs down the spinal cord, which together with the brain make up the central nervous system, then out through the nerves that make up the peripheral nervous system, which trigger the movement of muscles and the function of organs.

Voluntary movements are guided by the somatic system, which is made up of sensory and motor neurons. Sensory neurons take in information from our interaction with the world around us—touch, taste, sight, sound, smell—and relay it to the brain. Motor neurons go the other direction, sending information or instructions down through the spinal cord and into our muscle tissue, creating movement. You can think of it as a loop or a circuit—like arteries and veins. One sends blood from the heart to the body, the other sends blood from the body back to the heart.

Let's say you're walking down a city street. Your motor neurons tell your leg muscles to fire, your ankle to flex, and your foot to roll heel to toe, making a step. Your sensor neurons take in information about the unevenness of the sidewalk under your feet, the sound of the ambulance siren around the corner, the sight of the traffic light about to turn yellow, and the person coming from the other direction, headed right into your path. The brain processes this data in an instant and sends a set of commands to motor neurons that slow your pace and angle your hips. Your knees and feet follow by sidestepping a couple paces to the right to avoid the oncoming pedestrian.

The purpose of this little ninth-grade biology lesson is only to point out that, whether you realize it or not, you have conscious control of all the movements where the somatic system is activated. That is *not* the case with the autonomic system, which is the other half of our peripheral nervous system that controls involuntary movements: functions like heart rate, digestion, respiration, perspiration, and pupil dilation. This is important to note because this is the part of the nervous system that lights up like a Christmas tree under stress and in catastrophe.

Like the somatic system, the autonomic system is best understood in two parts: the sympathetic nervous system (SNS) and the parasympathetic nervous system (PSNS). The sympathetic nervous system governs your fight-or-flight response to external, physical threats and acute psychological stress. When you hear the gunshots at close range; when the proctor begins the exam, and you forget everything you studied; when the sky goes black and you hear the train whistle sound of an approaching tornado; when the spotlight hits your face and you have to deliver a speech to a packed house; and when you're standing between a mama bear and her cubs and she has you in her sights. This is when the sympathetic nervous system kicks in and dumps a bunch of adrenaline into your bloodstream. Your pupils and the secondary pathways in your lungs dilate, increasing visual acuity and lung capacity. Your heart rate, blood pressure, and respiration rate go way up, making your hands sweat. Your blood glucose spikes, and stored body fat gets released for more energy. Your skin goes pale while your face goes flush as the blood rushes to major muscle groups. All these bodily reactions are happening at once to facilitate the primal mobilization tactic in survival: fight or flight.

If the perceived threat persists beyond a moment or two, the brain then sends a signal to the adrenal glands to release cortisol—the body's primary stress hormone—to keep you on high alert. If the threat doesn't materialize (or when it ends), cortisol levels dissipate and the parasympathetic nervous system takes over to wind down the overall stress response and return the body's systems to normal. Whereas the SNS controls "fight or flight" in this capacity, it is said that the PSNS governs "rest and digest." And in that transitional phase when the body is catching up to the brain's understanding of the situation as the parasympathetic nervous system clears all the hormones from the bloodstream, it's not uncommon for someone to feel dizzy, nauseous, or exhausted.

Adapted over six million years of hominid evolution, this is how the human nervous system is supposed to work. But that's nowhere near the full story, right? None of us are so finely tuned to our nervous systems that our conscious actions perfectly sync up with the hormonal tsunami released into our bodies every time we're under stress. Often, there is a disconnect or delay between the instinct and the action, between the unconscious reaction and the conscious response. Building resilience is about bridging that disconnect and shrinking that delay as much as possible so that you will be able to act, when it counts, in time to save your life or the lives of the ones you love.

If you're reading this book, there's a good chance you or someone you know has experienced a traumatic event and discovered, in real time, that the disconnect was too wide, the delay too long. You neither fought nor fled . . . at least not quickly enough. Maybe, you froze. Or maybe, you've been lucky so far, and this is what you're worried will happen when catastrophe finally finds you. Like it did for the citizens at Virginia Tech University, on a normal day, in a routine schedule, on a beautiful spring morning.

TRAGEDY AT VIRGINIA TECH

Around 9:30 a.m. on April 16, 2007, a senior at Virginia Tech University named Seung-Hui Cho walked into Norris Hall—a classroom building on the north side of the school's campus—armed with two semiautomatic pistols, approximately four hundred rounds of hollow point ammunition, and heavy-duty chains with which he locked the building's three main doors from the inside. A few hours earlier, Cho had entered a residence hall across the campus where he had a student mailbox, found his way up to the fourth floor, then shot and killed a young female student and the resident assistant who came to her aid. It was shocking and frightening and horrifically tragic. And it was about to get much, much worse. For the next nine minutes, Cho would go from classroom to classroom on Norris Hall's second floor, firing methodically yet indiscriminately at students and teachers alike, targeting the rooms with the greatest number of people inside.

In room 206, a hydrology class, Cho stood in the doorway and shot and killed the instructor first, then nine of the thirteen students. Of the four survivors, two were injured, two were unharmed. Next, he entered room 207, a German-language class, and shot and killed the teacher and four students from the doorway, then walked down the aisle between rows of desks and shot six other students. This would be Cho's modus operandi for each of the classrooms he would ultimately enter: shoot from the doorway, walk up the aisles shooting students scrambling to hide, walk out into the hallway to reload, return to a classroom, and walk around the room once again, shooting those who were wounded but still alive or those he had missed the first time.

It would take a minute or two for students in nearby classrooms to register what was happening. Several students reported to investigators that they thought the gunshots were construction sounds or explosive reactions from chemistry lab experiments taking place on the first floor. The first 9-1-1 call came from room 211, a French-language class, where Cho went next. Students had barricaded the door with a number of desks, but Cho was able to push through them and enter the room. He shot and killed the teacher and the nearby student who had quickly pushed together the obstruction. Cho was then rushed by an ROTC cadet named Matthew La Porte, who was attempting to distract and disarm him. Cho shot La Porte seven times at close range, killing the twenty-year-old before walking silently up the aisles between desks, shooting students at very close range.

From room 211, Cho returned to room 206, killing a student who was wounded. He then tried to reenter room 207 and enter for the first time room 205, but failed on both counts because students had blocked the doors. (All six students in room 207 who'd previously been shot survived because four of them had barricaded the door with their wounded bodies.) Cho then returned to room 211, went up and down the aisles again, shooting those students who were still moving, before moving across and down the hall to room 204, an engineering class with sixteen students in attendance, where the professor, a seventy-seven-year-old Romanian Holocaust survivor named Liviu Librescu, held the door shut for as long as he could while his students fled out the second-story window, dropping into bushes and onto the lawn below. Eventually, Cho fatally shot Librescu through the door and forced his way into the classroom. Ten of the sixteen students had made it out the window by then. Four of the remaining six would be shot, one of whom would die.

The shooting began at 9:40 a.m. Police gained entry to the building through a side door at 9:50 a.m. and quickly converged on Cho's position. When Cho heard them coming, he walked back into room 211, where he'd returned most frequently and killed or injured the most people, and shot himself in the head. In the end, he'd attacked five classrooms—entering four, returning to at least two—and fired approximately 175 rounds, killing thirty-one people (twenty-five students, five teachers, and himself).* It would become the deadliest school shooting in the history of the United States.

FIGHT OR FLIGHT . . . OR FREEZE

A few feet away from Cho's body in room 211 lay Clay Violand. In a class of eighteen students, in which eleven were killed and six injured, Violand was the only one who survived unharmed. Like a few of his fellow classmates who survived after being shot, Violand had played dead. Unlike them, he played dead from the moment Cho first broke into the classroom.

*The total casualty count for the Virginia Tech shooting was fifty-six: thirty-three dead (thirty-one at Norris Hall including Cho, two at the residence hall), seventeen injured from gunshots, six injured from jumping out windows to escape.

"I wanted to go to the window," he told Amanda Ripley for her book *The Unthinkable: Who Survives When Disaster Strikes—and Why*, "but as soon as I saw the gun come in, I just froze." Violand collapsed in a heap behind his desk, landing on his side with his limbs twisted in unnatural directions. For those nightmarish nine minutes, while Cho was moving silently and murderously in and out of classrooms, Violand didn't move a muscle. "I tried to look as lifeless as possible," he said. "I remember thinking, 'he's going to shoot the moving people first.'" Violand was almost certainly right, because Cho came back into room 211 and, reloading as many as three times by Violand's count, put second and third rounds into wounded students who were still moving. He also put fresh rounds into those he'd missed the first time, cowering young men and women—kids, really—who were curled up in the fetal position, trying to hide, frozen with fear but clearly alive.

What's most interesting about Clay Violand's experience, from a physiological perspective at least, is what he was feeling as this horror was happening around him. The short explanation was . . . nothing. It was like he was paralyzed. "His whole body felt numb," Amanda Ripley described in her book, "as if all his limbs had fallen asleep." Something in Violand's mind told him to play dead, and his body had listened. Seung-Hui Cho clearly thought he looked dead, too. And in a way, you could say Violand really did feel dead. So much so that he was convinced, for a stretch of time, that he also must have been shot. Why else could he not move his arms and legs, or wiggle his fingers and toes?

The answer was: he truly did freeze. This freezing instinct is actually a third (and much less frequently discussed) facet of the fight-or-flight response that goes by a few different names: tonic immobility, thanatosis, and of course "playing dead." Like fight or flight, freeze is a survival instinct and reflexive fear response that is very effective when it's employed in the right circumstances. Weirdly, it is very poorly studied in humans.[*] It's mostly observed and studied in the wild. It's common in prey animals across the animal kingdom, from ants and frogs and snakes to ducks, rabbits, baby deer, and, most famously, possums—which is where we get the phrase "playing possum." When a prey animal senses imminent, inescapable danger from a predator, including humans, it might go limp, it might roll on its back with its eyes wide open and stiffen as if in rigor, it might even emit foul-smelling discharge, like the possum does, to mimic the stink of a rotting corpse. Some will play dead like this even when the predator has already attacked them, because further movement is likely to trigger additional (probably fatal) attacks and because most predators only go after live prey.

---

[*]If you put fight, flight, and freeze in the order they most frequently occur, most of the data point to "flight, freeze, or fight." Interestingly, "freeze" also sits in the middle of the spectrum between hyper- and hypoarousal, which are the states of the autonomous nervous system responsible for these stress responses.

Sounds eerily familiar, doesn't it? Very similar to what happened in room 211? Yes and no.

There's a pretty big difference between how the freeze response manifests in modern humans compared with the rest of the animal kingdom. Very rarely, in today's modern and technologically immersed world, does freezing happen to us the way it does for prey animals, or the way it did for Clay Violand. When we freeze in the face of a perceived threat, rarely does our body actually go limp or go numb to the point that we really look dead. The reason for that is, typically, most of our paralysis is mental, not physical. Yes, the shock of an overwhelming amount of stress makes our limbs feel like they weigh a thousand pounds, but we still *look* very much alive. Our minds, however, go blank. We struggle to communicate. We often dissociate like we're watching everything happen from outside our bodies.* We shut down. Someone like Seung-Hui Cho would never mistake us for dead, which goes a long way toward explaining how, of the thirty-one people he murdered in cold blood, twenty-eight were shot in the head, at close range, like an execution. Many of those unfortunate souls in Norris Hall had

---

*Out-of-body dissociation like this often occurs for victims of sexual assault and rape in the moment. It is a way for the mind to simultaneously compartmentalize the emotional trauma and numb the physical pain. Sadly, many victims—overwhelmingly women—report feeling deep shame for not fighting back, for "just lying there and letting it happen." Survivors are generally unaware that their tonic immobility was a natural, understandable, and ultimately successful survival instinct.

likely shut down. Their minds, not their bodies, had rooted them in place as everything got uprooted around them.

This is not how the fight-flight-freeze response is ideally supposed to work. So what's going on when this happens? The simplest way to put it is that the sympathetic nervous system is being overwhelmed. The stress is too great, the trauma too profound. So the parasympathetic nervous system shuts the whole thing down. Hard reboot. Another way to think about it is how the folks in the health education division at Harvard Medical School have described the relationship between the two parts: the sympathetic nervous system is the gas pedal, and the parasympathetic system is the brake. If we think of ourselves like cars, in moments of high stress it appears that the SNS hammers the accelerator and, if the sudden rush of fuel to the engine redlines it too quickly or keeps it pegged there for too long, the whole thing starts to feel like it's going to come apart, so the PSNS hits the brakes with both feet, locking up the wheels and killing the engine.

The upside is that the car still works. The downside is that it needs to be restarted . . . usually after cooling off for a bit. Unfortunately, in catastrophe, there is rarely time for a cooling-off period.

This isn't just a convenient analogy. There is robust data and modeling that support this relationship between stress and performance. It even has a name: the Yerkes-Dodson law*

---

*It's not really a law in the technical, scientific sense; that's just what they call it.

or the Yerkes-Dodson curve. Developed in the early twentieth century by a pair of psychologists, the idea is that performance increases, or gets better, with increased physiological or mental arousal (i.e., stress), *but only to a point*. After that point, as arousal continues to increase, performance plummets.

The original experiment by Yerkes and Dodson that teased out this relationship was done on mice. Since then, it's been applied to nearly every aspect of life—most often to workplace productivity—but almost never to survival and preparedness. When you do apply it, though, it perfectly explains the natural human struggle to respond effectively in a crisis.

The shape of everyone's Y-D curve is different. Some peak sooner. Some peak higher. Some fall away faster. But all curves are affected by the same three interrelated factors: complexity, familiarity, and confidence. In essence, the more complex the task you must complete in a highly stressful situation, the more likely your performance will suffer if you are unfamiliar with that specific task and/or you're not confident that you can complete it. In a case like that, the peak is lower and comes sooner, and the curve crashes quickly until it flatlines as the stress persists.

The one thing that stabilizes every curve, that neutralizes or equalizes the impact of complexity, familiarity, and confidence . . . is experience. Exposure. The less stress and discomfort you've experienced in your life, the greater the likelihood that you may shut down in a crisis. That's called fragility. The greater variety of stressors you have been exposed to, the

The Yerkes-Dodson Law
How anxiety affects performance

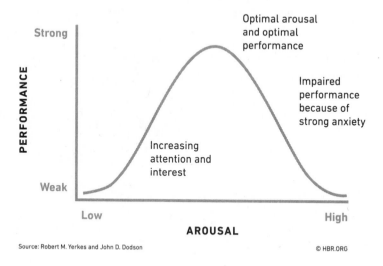

Source: Robert M. Yerkes and John D. Dodson

© HBR.ORG

more often you have been tested by the unfamiliar or the complex, the more likely you are to withstand a traumatic event and respond effectively. That is called resilience.

One of the primary goals of preparedness (and the purpose of everything I include in the rest of this book) is to give people different ways to build a wall right at that point in the curve where performance is about to diminish. That wall is like a callus on the hand of our sympathetic nervous system's response to adversity. It's a buffer against the engine running too hot, revving too fast for too long. That wall *is* resilience. Its building blocks are all the knowledge you gain and all the tools and skills you master while surviving difficult experiences that

The Yerkes-Dodson Law
How anxiety affects performance

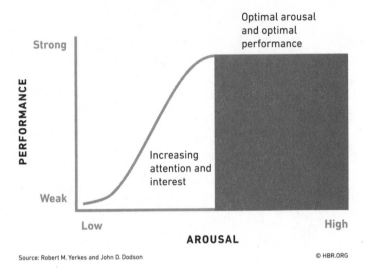

Source: Robert M. Yerkes and John D. Dodson © HBR.ORG

push you out of your comfort zone. The mortar is the confidence those experiences have given you—not just because you survived them but because you now know you can, *and will*, survive similar situations in the future.

When it's built well, resilience becomes more than just a wall or a barricade. It becomes almost like a living thing. It gathers momentum. It pushes further and further outward toward the extreme end of the arousal axis until the top of the performance curve is no longer a peak but a plateau. A new baseline, a better resting heart rate, for your ability to respond in a crisis, almost no matter how bad it gets.

EXPOSURE AND EXPERIENCE

Exposure is the key to building a resilient mindset because everyone, and I mean *everyone*, can freeze under stress, even the most hardened, combat-tested Special Operations operator. I've seen it with my own eyes. It has happened to me.

On my first combat deployment as a Green Beret, my unit was staging out of a tiny forward operating base in a valley in the middle of nowhere, Afghanistan. The location, while effective for making consistent contact with the enemy, was highly inconvenient for literally anything else. Everything required to make that base work had to be airlifted in, including water. One day we were getting a resupply of water and the pallet of heavy plastic water bottles tore free from its parachute as it slid out the back of the C-130 cargo plane high above. The pallet crashed down, outside the wire of our firebase, onto a helicopter landing zone (HLZ), scattering the bottles a couple hundred feet in every direction. As the team and some of our Afghan counterparts were out there collecting the water, a 107mm rocket came screaming into our position from somewhere on the surrounding hillside.

It was my first contact with enemy fire. Ever. And when that rocket came whistling in, I freaked out. I didn't cower in fear, but I scampered for cover and started to shake uncontrollably because, honestly, I didn't want to die. When the rocket exploded nearby, I started panicking. Every ounce of my being just wanted to hide, to be somewhere else. I was frozen for about three to six seconds. That doesn't sound like a long time, but in war that can be a lifetime. Many, many lifetimes if you consider how many bullets can be fired and how much ground a 107mm rocket can cover in that time.

I started yelling at my Afghan counterparts to get the hell off the HLZ, while the rest of my team tried to identify the direction of contact and set up defensive positions to engage the enemy. Seeing guys loaded down with water and other gear a few hundred yards from safety, I hopped on a four-wheeler and tore over to the outer fence line. I grabbed the interlocking loops of concertina wire with my bare hands to create an opening for them, gashing my palms pretty badly. In the moment, with the amplification of all my senses, I didn't feel any pain.

I wasn't frozen anymore. I was fighting. But upon reflection, it's clear I still wasn't fully in control of my response to the situation. I was in an extremely heightened state. My sympathetic nervous system was still flooring it and my parasympathetic system had its feet hovering over the brake. I was right at that point on the curve where, if you haven't built up that callus of resilience yet, performance falls away toward oblivion.

If you're wondering why a well-trained Green Beret might respond to that situation like I did, I'll tell you: I'd never trained for it. At Fort Bragg, North Carolina, we trained in small-unit tactics in the surrounding piney woodland around Camp

Mackall. We trained for close-quarters gunfights, ambushes with small-arms fire, and making contact with an unknown enemy set up in the tree line. We used artillery simulator rounds that had a high-pitch whistle and then a pop, like a firecracker, to simulate incoming mortar rounds and rockets.

None of that prepares you—or at least it didn't prepare me—for the chaos of real war; for being on the receiving end of a 107mm rocket, which sounds like a whistling freight train; for the concussive force when it explodes; for the fact that this dumb rocket, with no technology and no guidance system, can be fired off a rock anywhere on a mountain and has a kill radius of twenty-five meters. If the enemy were able to zero in on the HLZ, a bunch of our guys would have been evaporated by the impact. I trained to go on raids, to be the aggressor in war. Never in a million years did I think my first firefight would be against rocket ordnance coming out of the surrounding mountains while we were out in the open—which is the absolute worst place to be—picking up bottles of water like candy from a piñata.

My inexperience with this specific kind of engagement (i.e., lack of familiarity) is what froze me up. It was my exposure to all manner of stress and discomfort in training, as well as in my regular life as an outdoorsman and hunter, that fortified me (i.e., built confidence) against falling off the backside of that Y-D curve and quickly snapped me back to reality so I could perform the necessary (though admittedly not very complex) tasks to ensure my survival and that of my team.

If my time in Special Forces and my experiences in survival and preparedness has taught me anything, it's that it is impossible for a person to fully inoculate themselves against freezing up. What you *can* do, with experience, is shorten periods of paralysis to mere moments. Repeated exposure to stress can help you bridge the disconnect and cut the delay between the stimulus and your response.

A good example of what this looks like in practice are the quick, decisive actions of Matthew La Porte and Liviu Librescu on the morning of April 16, 2007. Separated in age by more than fifty years, raised a world apart from each other, these two men had something in common: exposure and experience. La Porte was an ROTC cadet. He had experience with guns. He was familiar and comfortable with the sound of gunfire, which can be deafening in confined spaces like a classroom. Librescu was a Holocaust survivor. He knew death. He had experience with indiscriminate psychopathic violence. Seeing people die in front of him was not new. Both men would heroically lose their lives, but the mental resilience they displayed in acting selflessly in response to Cho's rampage surely saved dozens of lives in Norris Hall.*

---

*Cho had more than two hundred rounds of unspent ammunition left in his backpack when Blacksburg police secured the scene. Without La Porte's and Librescu's efforts to fight Cho off, there's no telling how many of those bullets would have been fired.

TRAINING STRESS

Through exposure to stressful experiences, you can train to be able to do what Matthew La Porte did, what Liviu Librescu did, even what I did, in our respective moments of crisis. But what's most important is that you're able to do what's necessary in whatever uniquely stressful situation you find yourself in. The key is not just in the quantity of stress you expose yourself to, though—it's also the quality and variety. Right now, you could be living a life full of low-grade stress (most Americans are if you look at the data). It could even be high-grade stress—you could be redlining it every waking hour of every day. But if it's only one type of stress you experience, then even a modest amount of a totally unfamiliar kind of stress can catch you by surprise and freeze you up (take my word for it). Stress training starts by finding the edge of your comfort zones and learning how to adapt along the way.

If you're comfortable with different firearms platforms and you go to the range regularly to stay proficient, start practicing shooting on the move, in the dark, against a clock, or with someone shouting in your ear. Add variables like that to your firearms training—variables that are out of your control. Those variables create a new baseline and will exercise your technical skills while immersed in stress, which will expand what you can get away with. Remember, you won't rise to the occasion; you will fall to your level of training.

If you are a warm-weather person who hates the cold, start doing cold plunges. When the weather dips, take your dog for a walk in shorts and a T-shirt. If you hate the heat, do the opposite. Start using a dry sauna. Take your dog for a walk at high noon, wearing layers.

When you start to get really uncomfortable, when your palms start to sweat, and you can feel your pulse racing . . . sit with that feeling. I had a team sergeant who used to tell us to "embrace the suck," because the alternative is the suck embracing you. So embrace the discomfort. That's your sympathetic nervous system talking to you. Listen to it.

If you start to get overwhelmed and feel yourself shutting down, there are two simple tactics to employ: conscious breathing and positive self-talk. Stop, take in a big breath, hold it, big breath out, pause, repeat. When you feel yourself coming back to earth, start telling yourself, *I can do this. I got this. I know what to do.* Repeat. Say it out loud so you can hear it, not just think it. It might sound a little woo-woo, like we're in a meditation class at a yoga retreat, but it works. I know, because it's exactly what I did as I hunkered down after that 107mm rocket exploded. I took a couple deep breaths, told myself, *Mike, you got this, you know what to do,* and six seconds later my head was back in the game. Not only will you reap the benefits of the off-gassing of carbon dioxide, allowing oxygen back into your brain, but just the conscious thought of breathing will plug you back into reality.

Being able to pull yourself together like this under stress is of the utmost importance. It's at least as important, if not more so, than knowing exactly what to do in a crisis, because in the modern world many of the actions we must take in an emergency to save our lives require fine motor skills. We're thousands of generations past the primitive instinct to simply run away or to attack with our fists. We need to be able to dial 9-1-1 and relay lifesaving information on a mobile phone, put a key into a locked door or a car's ignition, draw a pistol from a concealed carry under stress, or assess the bleed and apply a tourniquet. Each of these tasks requires mental and physical dexterity—both of which leave us when our sympathetic nervous system has swamped us in stress hormones. Without training, without exposure or experience, when our hands can't stop shaking, when we can't feel anything, these are just some of the simple lifesaving tasks that become next to impossible to perform.

THE ENDS OF THE BELL CURVE

I once gave a Preparedness 101 speech to a group at a rodeo in Montana. It's from a program I started called Responsible Citizens where we teach free training to citizens across the country in all fields of preparedness. After the speech, a man and his wife came up to me. They were dressed like vacationing investment bankers and definitely a little out of their element in rural Montana. The man said to me, "We're both in our forties, and we've never done anything like the stuff you've done, but we want to be resilient like you. What should we do?" It was a tough question, because within the scope of preparedness, they were way behind. But that didn't mean it was too late for them to start, even if they were starting from zero.

"Have you ever been camping?" I asked them. Neither of them had. "Go camping, just for a weekend," I said. I told them to find a real spot, not an RV park or a glamping resort, but also not some place so remote that county search and rescue might have to come and pull them out of a ravine. Once they found a spot, I told them to bring only the essentials. No toothbrushes, no coffeemaker, no propane stove, no deodorant or makeup or memory foam pillow. Then I told them not to leave the area. They could hike or scavenge for kindling and firewood, but this was not a vacation—this was training.

The couple got very nervous at the mere idea of it all. They started to negotiate conditions with me, right there on the spot. They hadn't even felt the hard ground under their sleeping bags or the cold morning air waiting for them outside their tents, and already they were getting anxious. I reassured them and gave them some suggestions for camping spots near where they lived, but I have no idea if they actually followed my guidance. I hope they did.

After that encounter, I started to use camping as an introductory part of my survival and preparedness courses. I realized that no amount of firearms training, emergency medicine training, defensive driving, or home security training was going to be effective if people didn't have a basic level of resilience. If they hadn't built up even a little bit of a callus on their sympathetic nervous system. And many people haven't. Especially in the United States, there are a lot of people who exist permanently on either end of the Yerkes-Dodson curve. Most, I would argue, exist on both ends at once—by which I mean they have little to no experience with, or exposure to, physical stress and discomfort; at the same time they live in a perpetual state of heightened psychological stress. They are mentally fried and physically atrophied. It's a recipe for disaster . . . especially in a catastrophe.

I'm not blaming those people for their predicament, to be perfectly clear. It's not totally their fault. One of the big problems ordinary people face when it comes to preparedness and survival is that modern civilized society has made it harder to achieve a basic level of resilience. It's done this, ironically enough, by trying to make everyone's lives *easier*. All of the technological advancements, all of the luxuries and creature comforts—pretty much everything that has been labeled "progress" over the last seventy-five years—have had one main goal: removing existential risk and physical discomfort from our regular, everyday lives. We *want* to be safer. We *want* things to be easier. And rightly so. But that convenience has come at a high cost: lack of preparedness for the irregular, for the anomalous, and for the once-in-a-lifetime catastrophic event.

How do you train for the worst-case scenario in a world set on eliminating it from your life or insulating you from it when elimination isn't possible? If iron sharpens iron, how do you get hardened when you've been forged in cotton candy? You do it by ripping apart those sweet, sugary threads constricting you like concertina wire and creating an opening to step through, to continually test yourself, to prove that you can endure discomfort, persevere in the face of stress, and come out the other side prepared for worse. That is the resilient mindset, and that is the first step in being ready for anything.

Bottom line: start getting comfortable at being uncomfortable and you will be more than okay.

2

PLANNING

As a society we have grown comfortable with outsourcing our lives for the sake of convenience. If the faucet leaks, we call a plumber. If our neighbor breaks our fence, we call a lawyer, then a carpenter. If our car breaks down, we call a mechanic, then an Uber.

Police, fire, EMS, education, the courts, supermarkets, mobile apps, government policies, public utilities, manufacturing—each of these institutional forces exists to provide us with things we want or need that we cannot easily get for ourselves. And this is fine when things are going well and times are good. That's just what it looks like when a cooperative society is working the way it's supposed to.

But what about when catastrophe strikes? When institutions have collapsed and services have been crippled by diminishing resources? Or when politics take priority over responding to citizens in harm's way? When finding safety and security becomes entirely your responsibility? What then? Do you know what to do? Who to call? What to bring? Where to go? How to get there?

If you don't, if everything I just said has dialed your anxiety and your heart rate up, then most likely it's because you don't have a plan for when things go bad.

You need a plan.

You need to know *how to make a plan*, which means you need to understand how to plan for contingencies. To not only line out how to respond in a catastrophe efficiently and effectively, but also how to shift your actions and adapt along the way. The number one characteristic common to all survivors of catastrophe is adaptability. And the best course of action for becoming adaptable is to have a plan for a series of predetermined contingencies in your back pocket.

In Special Operations, at least a third of the proposed timeline of every mission is spent in the planning phase. When we plan, we never plan for things to go right. Instead, we always plan for things to go wrong. What I mean is, we expect to accomplish our objective, but we never expect that the *way* we intend to accomplish it will go off without a hitch. It's called Murphy's *law* for a reason.

In war or in a fight, there are no rules, really. And your opponent is never going to make it easy on you. They're going to booby-trap the most obvious attack route and block the most obvious escape route. They aren't constrained or limited by the rule of law, or a scheduled timeline, or approval from up the chain of command. With flexibility and the right motivation, the enemy most certainly is going to make your life a living hell.

But it's not always an adversary who creates these obstacles. It can be the elements or your lack of equipment or your own biases and preconceptions. In chaos and uncertainty, these are the forces that often work against you, at the worst possible moment.

Whether you're at war with yourself, Mother Nature, or an angry mob, you need to be prepared to operate at the speed of war, and that requires a sound plan.

HOW TO START PLANNING

Every plan in preparedness begins with a simple conversation—with your spouse, with your kids, maybe just with yourself. Imagine you're sitting in the kitchen; it's after work and you're having a glass of wine with your spouse. You have a clear view to the front door, and you nod in that direction:

> *Hey honey, what would you do if a guy burst through our front door right now?*
>
> Well, I'd kick his ass.
>
> *Okay, but what if he has a gun?*
>
> I'd take cover, draw my pistol, and defend our lives.
>
> *Are you carrying yours right now?*
>
> No.
>
> *Where is it?*
>
> Upstairs on the dresser like it always is when we're at home.
>
> *Do you think you could get to it before he could get to me?*

This conversation is about one specific aspect of home preparedness, and yet, like every other aspect of preparedness, the dialogue could go on forever, following an infinite branching chain of if-then scenarios like a lethal "choose your own adventure" game. Still, this little snippet produces a few important questions that will need to be answered to craft the most robust home preparedness plan possible. (We'll talk all about homestead preparedness in Chapter 7.)

- How strong are our door locks?

- Is the path from the front door to the kitchen too open?

- Is there a better or ideal place to store a firearm?

- Could we have had better security measures in place to give us an earlier warning?

- How likely is something like this to happen based on where we live?

All these questions and the countless others we could come up with are important and should not be glossed over. We must treat each question as a proposed problem and navigate all potential solutions. In the military decision-making process, we call this "course of action development," otherwise known as war gaming. It's a deliberate exercise that takes place in an isolated facility, where the entirety of the team's effort is focused on identifying and drilling down into all—and I mean all—the potential outcomes for a proposed action. It's an exhaustive process we go through at our version of the kitchen table to flush out all potential deficiencies in our planning.

When we analyze catastrophe and why some people live and some people die, we can begin to increase probabilities by weighing risk and outcomes. What is the risk of a particular catastrophic event occurring, and what is the probability that, if I'm not sufficiently prepared, it may result in major injury or death? The game is to increase the statistical probability of survival based on our understanding of existing data and implementing a sound plan.

Think about motor vehicle accidents. Americans drive approximately three *trillion* miles every year. In 2020, 38,824 people died on America's roads. That's 1.34 fatalities per 100 million miles driven, or 106 people every day. When it comes to preparedness, there is one group to which these statistics are more relevant than any other: truck drivers.

Truck drivers drive more miles per capita than any other group out on the road, *by far*. The average trucker covers up to three thousand miles per week, many of those miles on highways where speeds regularly exceed seventy miles per hour (aka "the death zone"). There are millions of people living in cities (such as Manhattan, or Mumbai, or Mexico City) who haven't driven three thousand miles in their entire adult lives, if they even own a car at all. Comparatively, the probability that a trucker will be involved in or witness a major motor vehicle accident is astronomically high. If there's one group that should be well-prepared for catastrophic car wrecks—heavily invested in defensive driving skills, with a good first aid kit mounted in their rigs—it's truck drivers. (We'll talk a lot more about first aid kits for vehicles in Chapter 6.) But urban city dwellers? Maybe not so much. Their preparedness resources would be better deployed toward things that are much more common in urban environments (e.g., muggings, civil unrest, terrorist attacks).

Similarly, consider earthquakes. There's roughly one 8+ magnitude earthquake somewhere in the world every year. A magnitude 9+ earthquake happens approximately one to three times per century. These are the kinds of quakes that topple bridges, collapse homes, and demolish infrastructure. That means if you live to be eighty years old, which is about the average life span for a healthy person in the developed world, you're likely to live through eighty huge earthquakes. That seems like a lot. Enough that we should all be seriously prepared. Except context matters here.

Nearly all deadly seismic activity occurs in the known seismic zones around the Pacific Ocean and in Central Asia, with a significant portion of it happening under the ocean itself. So, if you live in California or Japan or in cities within a couple days' drive of the Himalayas or the Hindu Kush, you should definitely have a good flashlight, bottled water, and practice running into doorways or ducking under desks. But if you live in Florida or Scandinavia or Malta or Qatar (all places with incredibly minor and infrequent seismic activity), you probably shouldn't waste time or money preparing for "The Big One." You'd be much better off preparing for hurricanes or blizzards or heat waves and drought—because those *will* happen more frequently precisely where you live, and while they are less deadly on average, your increased exposure to them will increase the probability that you end up in the middle of one of the bad ones.

It's impossible to be prepared for anything and everything, but it's very possible to be prepared for everything that has any real chance of happening based on where you live, what you do for work, and how you live your life. Before you start building your actual preparedness plans, spend time thinking about which things you absolutely must be prepared for. Spend time talking with those who will be a part of your plan about whether, and to what extent, they currently feel prepared. Use that conversation to stress-test their assumptions and to do an inventory of the equipment and skills you'll need to make the plan you ultimately construct as successful as possible.

SET YOUR PACE

In the military and in emergency response circles, there is a redundancy preplanning system, called PACE, that is designed to keep people, units, and elements connected to each other out in the field, even (or especially) when things are going sideways. It's an acronym:

P—Primary

A—Alternate

C—Contingency

E—Emergency

As a methodology, it is the agreed-upon and mutually understood progression of communication modalities that each member of a team or unit can move through to make contact with any other member. In layman's terms, it's the backup plan to the backup plan to the backup plan. So, for instance, in the case of something like a FEMA team in a disaster area establishing a comms plan with the headquarters element, maybe the Primary mode is a dedicated radio frequency on an RF band. If that channel is supercluttered with higher-priority traffic, maybe the Alternate is a different, more general frequency that only requires the turn of a dial. If that isn't available, maybe the Contingency is a switch to cellular phones. And if that doesn't work, then maybe the Emergency is sending a messenger to deliver the information in person.

While designed initially for redundancy in communications and first aid, the PACE protocol is also an ideal way to conceive a survival and preparedness plan because, as I just mentioned, in an emergency situation your first (primary) instinct—typically the most obvious or most direct—is rarely available to you.

For the purpose of illustrating how a PACE plan can come together, let's use a two-story suburban house fire as the event we're planning for. It's the middle of the night, and your two kids are asleep, each in their own bedroom. Your family dog, who is usually sleeping at the foot of your bed, is barking hysterically down the hall. You wake up, and immediately you smell smoke. You get up to investigate and see a raging fire that a basic home fire extinguisher (Do you have one? Where is it stored?) would never be able to put out. What next?

Primary

Your first choice is always the easiest and most direct path to safety, which in the case of a house fire is most likely heading down the stairs and out the front door.

So, Primary = front door.

But it's not always that easy. We also must remember that our children, who lack experience, advanced cognitive decision-making, and fully developed frontal lobes, need to have conditioned responses. They need to have programmed and rehearsed means of activating their movement—especially while under stress. This applies to the dog as well.

As infantrymen, we develop these tactics through battle drills to speed up individual reaction time to the enemy and minimize lull time. Similarly, your children must be trained and conditioned for this primary course of action in the PACE plan to work. One way to do this is to use audible alarms or procedure words (or prowords for short), which are basically verbal versions of condensed Morse code commands that signify it's time to move. So, let's say you're initiating the P in your PACE plan, you would yell "Irene!" Because you've planned and rehearsed using this proword, your children and your dog know immediately to move to the front door and out of the house to a predetermined rendezvous point.

The PACE plan often initiates action, but there are more complexities depending on how many people you are responsible for, and how their age, physical condition, experience, and history with stressful events tend to affect their ability to respond and act quickly.

Alternate

Alternate = back door.

Now, let's assume that the path to the front door is blocked by smoke. Maybe *you* could make it, but with young kids who are scared and inexperienced, you don't want to risk them freezing up or accidentally inhaling too much smoke. So you make a shift to the other ground-floor exit.

Have a backup proword for an immediate and alternate plan of action. You should rehearse this route with your kids as well. Not just so they can get familiar with it, but also so they can know it instinctively and act on it automatically if you're not there to announce the proword yourself when it becomes clear that they've got to move to the back door. Maybe you're out of town, maybe you're still upstairs helping their frail, bedridden grandmother. There are a million reasons you might not be there in that moment. Why you're not there is unimportant; what matters is understanding that in the absence of sufficiently clear information and the trained ability to problem solve, stress builds very quickly, and it could trigger a freeze response in your children.

The simple way to initiate this rehearsal of the pivot to the alternate plan is to have the conversation with your child as you're walking to the front door as part of practicing the primary phase of the plan.

"Kiddo, if I'm not here and the front door is blocked by the fire, where are you going?" Let them answer. Prompt them if necessary, but then let them navigate both of you to the back door. Let them use their own creativity to source the solution. It will help them feel more invested in the creation of the plan, and it will help them become more adaptive and less rigid under stress.

Contingency

The layout of your home is a major factor in how a fire PACE plan gets made. For instance, thick smoke at the top of the stairs could thwart your primary (front door) and your alternate (back door) routes if you only have that one stairwell. Which means now you're looking at a less convenient contingency— a more direct and probably more risky means of escape, but that's why it's the backup to the backup.

Contingency = master bedroom window

When you've moved into the back half of a PACE plan, you know things are getting tricky. It may force you to reprioritize on the fly. For instance, if you're going out a second-story window, responsibility for the dog may shift to you because it will require greater upper body strength to carry and control the animal out the window.

But more importantly, once you've established your contingency route as part of the planning process, you then need to establish whether you have everything you need for that route to be accessible. What does that mean in the context of our hypothetical two-story house fire?

- Do you have a fire ladder?

- Is it stored nearby? Who's in charge of getting it? Who's in charge of deploying it?

- Do you know how to unlock and open your windows?

- Are they old? Which ones are painted shut? Which ones don't stay open on their own?

- Do you have storm windows or screens? Do you know how to remove them?

- If the windows do not open, do you have a glass breaker and blanket to minimize the risk of injury while escaping?

It's not enough to know that you'll go out the window if the front and back doors are inaccessible. You need to know *which* window; you need to know how to open it; and you need to be confident that it will open in the first place. That's why rehearsals are so important.

Of all the elements of a PACE plan, it's often this one that needs to be maintained and trained most regularly. Everyone knows how to run down the stairs and open a door. Not everyone has experience climbing out a window and down a chain ladder.

Emergency

We all know that familiar phrase stenciled on those metal-and-glass cases mounted to the walls inside large buildings. They hold a fire extinguisher, an alarm handle, an ax, or a length of coiled hose.

IN CASE OF EMERGENCY
BREAK GLASS

In building your PACE plan, it's highly likely that that is precisely what you'll be doing, either literally or figuratively. This is your method of last resort. It's the riskiest route, but probably the closest—and maybe the *only* route—given your lack of options.

Emergency = closest window, by any means necessary

Maybe it's a second-floor window at the back of the house that drops into some bushes. Maybe it's through a dormer window and onto the roof at the end of the house, opposite from where the fire is. Maybe it's onto the roof and then over to the limb of a large overhanging tree (assuming you know that those windows will open).

If there's time, maybe the plan is that you jump down or scale the downspout, then race to get a ladder from the garage that the rest of your family can use. But then, that raises another set of questions, right? Do you have a ladder? Is it tall enough? Is it accessible from outside your house? Part of the planning process is to answer those questions and solve those problems in advance.

It's important to remember that once you've reached the last, emergency phase of a PACE plan, there are usually no great options. They're all suboptimal, some riskier and more dangerous than others. In the case of a house fire escape plan, your job is to scout your home to identify every possible way you and your family might be able to get out when the doors and the ground-floor windows are blocked.

Get creative. Accept the risks involved. There should be no expectation that you're going to get out unscathed. The goal at this point is just *to survive*.

ARROGANCE AND WILLFUL IGNORANCE ARE YOUR ENEMY

Every good preparedness plan requires good information. You must know your immediate surroundings and the larger environment through which you will most likely have to navigate. You need to understand your adversary—whether that's a single active shooter, a mob of angry protesters, a pathogen, or something like a fire or freezing temperatures. You need to have a good grip on the tools and equipment you might be able to utilize. And you need to have an honest accounting of what you can and cannot do—physically, in terms of stamina and strength;

mentally, in terms of tough decisions with hard choices; and tactically, in terms of skills and abilities.

We've talked about how to distill this kind of information through conversation and evaluation. And you might think that the greatest impediment to a good plan is the lack of sufficient information when you don't have these evaluative conversations. After all, how can you deal effectively with all possible contingencies in each circumstance if you don't know enough to identify what those contingencies might be or whether you're equipped to handle them? But lack of information isn't the biggest problem. Don't get me wrong, it's not great and it sucks to deal with, but I would be lying if I didn't acknowledge that sometimes even the smallest amount of information can be enough to pull together a workable plan.

The biggest enemies of good planning are arrogance and ignorance. It's the foolish belief, on the one hand, that you don't need a plan for catastrophe because "that will never happen to me"; and it's the refusal, on the other hand, to even consider planning for the worst-case scenario because you don't like to think about all the bad things that can happen in the world. It's difficult to know which of these is worse or more common—ignorance or arrogance—because in the end the result is the same. It's the difference between having your head in the sand or up your ass—either way, you won't be able to see what's coming or which way to go when it gets here.

Arrogance

History is filled with examples of arrogance being the demise of people in a crisis. Maybe the most famous one occurred in April 1912 when the RMS *Titanic* left the docks in Southampton, England, on its maiden voyage to New York with more than 2,200 people aboard (including crew) but only enough lifeboats (20) for about 1,200. There were a few reasons this happened. For one, the owners, the White Star Line company, wanted to preserve as much deck space as possible for guests to walk and lounge on, and lifeboats took up lots of deck space. Second, they were in compliance with maritime law, which required only sixteen lifeboats for a ship the size of the *Titanic*, so they didn't technically *need* more lifeboats. But third, and most importantly, no one involved with the design and construction of the ship thought any of that stuff mattered because they were convinced the ship was unsinkable.

That arrogance doomed *Titanic* passengers because it trickled down into countless other aspects of how the ship was run. It gave management the delusional confidence to order the captain to steam through the icy waters of the North Atlantic at ridiculously dangerous speeds (for a boat). It gave members of the crew such a false sense of security that neither the lookout post, called the crow's nest, nor the bridge had a pair of binoculars to see danger coming. Worst of all, such arrogance resulted in the formulation of no meaningful evacuation procedures, no emergency response plans, and even less training.

On April 14, 1912, in the middle of a moonless night, the *Titanic* hit an iceberg, and then the shit hit the fan. Chain of command immediately and completely broke down. The crew, with little sense of what to do or in what order, made some horrible decisions that cost hundreds of lives. One crew member locked the third-class passengers down in the bowels of the ship until the first-class passengers could reach and board the lifeboats. Other crew members who were manning those lifeboats then only filled them to 60 percent to 70 percent capacity, because they weren't sure that the cranes used to lower lifeboats into the water, called davits, could support that much weight. They were worried that the davits would collapse, and the lifeboats would tumble into the sea. They were worried because they'd had little to no lifeboat training, and they hadn't been told by management that the davits had been successfully tested at maximum capacity back in port.

The result was a total catastrophe. Of the 2,224 people aboard the *Titanic*, only 706 survived. That is 472 fewer than the total number of lifeboat seats available, and 1,500 fewer than should have survived. The arrogance of a few led to the death of many, when a basic set of emergency plans and a little bit of training could have saved nearly everyone.

Ignorance

As dangerous as it is to rely entirely on the infrastructure of society to protect and provide for you, living in denial about the randomness of misfortune and being willfully ignorant about the possibility that someday you might have to protect and provide for yourself is courting disaster. We all know people who live like this. They don't believe that bad things could *never* happen to them, like arrogant people do, but they believe (or maybe a better word is *hope*) that they can insulate themselves from bad things by eliminating as much risk from their lives as possible. Remember, hope is never a course of action.

To an extent, they're right. You don't have to worry about knowing the cutaway procedures for a malfunctioning parachute or how to safely fall from a height if you never go skydiving or bungee jumping. You don't need to worry about getting lost or having a wilderness survival plan if you never go hiking or camping. But what I'm talking about goes beyond those discrete cases where eliminating a sufficient amount of risk in a particular area makes having emergency plans no longer necessary. I'm talking about the kind of person who believes that making plans in the first place increases the chance that bad things will occur because you're tempting fate when you do it.

This is absolute nonsense, obviously. But tell me you don't know someone who acts exactly like this. We all do! The wealthy aunt who doesn't have a will because she doesn't like to think about death. The stubborn father who won't go to the doctor for that mole on his back because he's afraid of what they're going to tell him. The goofy friend who is all about karma and good vibes and doesn't want to let any of that dark, negative energy into their house. These people exist, and many of them are important to us, which is why it's important to make the point: you cannot wish away catastrophe and you cannot hide from it, not completely. You can only prepare for it so that when it comes, it doesn't kill you.

PLANNING FOR THE UNPLANNABLE

As important as proper planning is to a fully prepped life, there are some things you just can't plan for. There's no PACE plan for the unforeseeable. But what you can do is embed the principles of PACE planning into how you walk through the world. There's something magical about planning that doesn't have anything to do with the plan itself, but with what you learn in the process of making the plan. That's where the gold nuggets lie.

A simple way to picture what that could look like is to think back to every mafia movie or spy thriller you've ever seen and to remember that one scene (they almost all have a version of this scene) where the main character enters a restaurant with a group and insists on sitting in the corner facing the door. They do this because they want to be able to see the entire room so they can't be snuck up on and killed. In their line of work, that kind of catastrophic event has a relatively high probability of occurring, and they don't want to be caught unaware or with their guard down.

What often goes unsaid in those scenes, but is implied, is

that they have also cased the entire place. They know where the likely threats would come from, and they've identified every means of escape, likely in descending order of efficiency. This is to say, they have a loosely constructed, impromptu PACE plan for if things kick off.

You can imagine a version of this happened in room 204 in Norris Hall: Liviu Librescu's classroom. Librescu was a resilient man who knew catastrophe. When Seung-Hui Cho started bursting into neighboring classrooms and opening fire, it's not hard to believe that Librescu knew the closest stairwell was one room away to the left, the other stairwell was three rooms down to the right, and neither was accessible, based on the sound of the gunfire. So he guided his students to the next best option— the second-floor window—while he barricaded the door with his body. Librescu, whether he realized or not, had a PACE plan.

So can you. You can do the same thing. Every building you enter, every room you step into, you can casually note where all the exits are. Which one's closest? Which one gets you outside fastest? Are there windows? Do they open? If you want to take it a little further, look at your phone and see what the cell service is like. Are fire extinguishers nearby? What about a defibrillator?

With a little bit of training and practice, you can do this kind of room scan and have your own makeshift PACE plan in less than thirty seconds. And the best part, from a preparedness perspective, is that this planning discipline has huge second- and third-order effects. It makes you more resilient, because you'll be contemplating all types of worst-case scenarios and less likely to be shocked or paralyzed by them; and it heightens your situational awareness, because you'll constantly be conscious of your immediate physical surroundings. When it comes to putting yourself in the best position to survive the worst day of your life, you can't ask for much more than that.

3

SITUATIONAL AWARENESS

Before you read another word, I want you to grab a piece of paper and a pen. Now I want you to think about your daily commute, or if you work from home, the route you drive or walk most often. Maybe it's dropping the kids off at school. Maybe it's walking to school yourself. The route itself doesn't matter. I want you to think back to the last time you did that drive or took that walk.

Now, I want you to pick up your pen and write down everything you remember from that trip. Not the stuff you know is there because you've memorized the route—the Starbucks on the corner, the church with the hand-lettered sign, things like that. I'm talking about the details that you can recall from that specific trip.

If you're anything like 99.9 percent of daily commuters in the United States, your list has fewer items than this chapter has paragraphs so far.

This should terrify you.

If you were driving, it means you were piloting five thousand pounds of steel and fiberglass, quite often at deadly speeds, and you have no real, conscious idea what happened between the time you pulled out of your driveway and the time you pulled into your destination.

If you were walking, especially if you are in a decent-size city, it means you navigated a gauntlet of uneven sidewalks, speeding cars and trucks, construction zones, animals, and strangers with unknown intentions—but you wouldn't be able to tell an investigator anything if you found out the following day that someone had been carjacked and kidnapped half a block behind you.

This kind of obliviousness and conscious disconnection is an epidemic in the developed world. Because we have faith in the rule of law, because we have become a self-obsessed culture, because we have come to expect that every institution in our society is always making our lives as safe as possible, we tend to waltz through the world daily without a single, solitary clue. We run seemingly on autopilot, bouncing randomly between distractions and stimuli like a Roomba sweeping our kitchen floors.

If you want to be prepared, if you don't want to be caught completely off guard when the worst-case scenario comes to pass, then you need to be always actively conscious of your surroundings. The term for that—for conscious observation of your environment—is "situational awareness."

If building a resilient mindset is the thing that will help you survive the immediate shock of catastrophe, and having a proper plan is the thing that will help you survive and escape that catastrophe, developing good situational awareness is the thing that will give you the best shot at avoiding catastrophe in the first place.

THE SPIKE IN THE GRAPH

As a teacher of preparedness, I know that situational awareness is both the trickiest and the simplest thing to talk about. Initially, everyone wants to know the specific things they should always be looking out for. It doesn't matter if they're walking into a bar, visiting a new city, or trekking into the wilderness. *How can I tell if there's a threat in this place? How can I tell if I'm in a dangerous neighborhood? How can I tell if there are bears or mountain lions or rattlesnakes in my vicinity?* These are the kinds of questions you might have as you first begin to wrestle with your own situational awareness. Unfortunately, there is no clean or complete answer to any of them. The answer is always "It depends."

It depends, because what you're looking for in any situation is anything out of the ordinary. You're trying to spot the anomaly, the guy going up the down escalator, or as I call it, the spike in the pattern. The thing is, the only way to reliably know if something is out of the ordinary is to understand what is ordinary for that situation. You must know the natural shape of the pattern before you can confidently determine whether what you're witnessing is a spike off it.

Yousef Badou, a former Marine infantryman and now one of the preeminent experts on situational awareness, calls this "setting your baseline." It's a concept he became familiar with while winning hearts and minds and doing counterinsurgency operations overseas. His unit was in the thick of it in Iraq during a very active, very deadly time in the war. He and his team were responsible for patrolling several towns and villages on a weekly cycle. They'd come through in a convoy, meet with village elders to hear their problems or take their requests, and try to establish a working relationship. All without getting ambushed or blown up by improvised explosive devices (IEDs).

"We'd roll into these towns and everyone there would hate us. Week after week, it was complete hatred. That was our baseline for these towns," Yousef described to me in 2021. If his unit rolled through and everyone stared daggers at them, that meant everything in that town was operating as normal.

"Then one day we'd roll through, and like usual everyone hated us, but now there was this one guy up ahead smiling at us, waving for us to come over," Yousef recalled, "and *that* is the chucklehead I want to talk to."

Why? Because he didn't fit the baseline. He was going up the down escalator. He spiked the pattern. If you were going to place bets on where the biggest threat in that village was most likely to come from, the smiling villager waving his arms would be even money.

It's important to remember that the baseline of every situation is different. What you're looking for in a restaurant is different from what you're looking for in a stadium, which is different from what you're looking for in nature, in a crowded city block, in a small town in Iraq, or in any number of different scenarios. And the only way to get really good at both establishing these different baselines and identifying spikes off them is with experience. To be prepared for what the world can throw at you, you have to spend time out in the world.

The extent to which your situational awareness can be sharpened and effective is limited by the extent of your life experience. If you grew up in a small town in Idaho and you've never left there, when you come to New York City for the first time, your situational awareness is going to be poorly calibrated and wildly inefficient because everything around you will feel like a spike off the baseline of your limited experience. It's going to take you a couple days to figure out the baseline for all those Manhattan environments, just like it took Yousef a couple months going through those Iraqi villages before he could feel confident that he had his head wrapped around things.

But even when different physical environments are similar, their baselines can often be quite unique. The baseline of a Monday morning Delta flight from Atlanta to New York City is very different from that of a Friday night JetBlue flight from New York City to Las Vegas. They're both 737s run by major American airlines traveling between big cities, but the people on those flights are going to be very different and traveling for very different reasons. Which means if you hear raucous commotion back in row 27 of the JetBlue flight, it's probably just some drunk young people pre-partying for "Vegas, baby, Vegas." But if you hear a similar type of commotion on that Delta flight, you're definitely going to want to pay attention, because that kind of behavior is way out of the ordinary for a Monday morning flight full of business travelers. In other words, it's a spike in the pattern screaming *Look at me! Look at me!*

A spike is your indication that something is off. It may not be bad in the end, but you won't know that until . . . well, you know. So acknowledge the spike when you see it and keep it in the back of your mind as you engage with the people around you and navigate through your environment, because if there is a threat it's going to come from one of those two sources—the people or the environment—often in combination.

THE ENVIRONMENT

When we talk about the environment in this context, we don't necessarily mean nature—though anyone who has survived a forest fire or a natural disaster knows that nature is definitely not to be ignored. Rather, what we mean is your immediate physical surroundings. The apartment you live in, the neighborhood you're walking in, the restaurant you're sitting in, the club you're partying at, the office building you're working in, the gym you're watching your kids play basketball in, the school where they go every weekday. The physical composition of these spaces and your physical orientation within them are the main variables in the threat equation that defines the relative safety of your environment—or more exactly, *your* safety relative to your environment.

The question, then, becomes how best to assess these spaces. How do you figure out whether your immediate surroundings are safe or they pose a threat? And then, how do you *make yourself* safer in those spaces?

Finding the answers to those questions begins with knowing how to look. With a few exceptions across cultures, sight is understood to be the most powerful human sense. Most of us are able to communicate about what we see, for instance, better than we can communicate about what we hear, touch, taste, or smell. Because of this, we generally consider ourselves to be good observers. It's one of the reasons we love stuff like *Where's Waldo?* and those "spot the difference" games. We think we're good at them. But we're not. Just because you can *see* perfectly doesn't mean you know how to *look* at things well.

Our lackluster observational skills aren't totally our fault. Yes, our false sense of visual confidence tends to make us lazy with how we take in our surroundings (we think we're just going to immediately spot the important stuff), but also, it's incredibly difficult for the human eye to take in a lot of textured visual information all at once and process it thoroughly. As a result, what we really end up doing when we look at something is taking fuzzy two-dimensional snapshots of it and then unconsciously allowing our memories (of that specific place or places like it) to fill in the blanks and sharpen the detail of the image we've just captured. This means that when we look at a busy street, the bleachers in a baseball stadium, a crowded restaurant, a forested hillside, we rarely ever see what's really there. Instead, we create a composite image that *approximates* reality and use that to make judgments and decisions about our safety.

We all do this. Every day, with everything. It's what allows us to drive to work or walk to school without having to be super focused or on high alert. And that's perfectly fine under ordinary circumstances and when we're not under stress. To do it any other way would put us under an unsustainable cognitive load. We'd be exhausted, and eventually the hard drive that is our mind would crash. But in extraordinary circumstances, when stress peaks and the stakes are high, like with catastrophe or in an emergency? Approximating the reality of your environment in those situations isn't going to cut it. To be situationally aware of potential threats emanating from our environment, we can't lean on old, unconscious habits like that. We have to build new, conscious habits. We have to learn how to *actively observe*. We have to learn how to see systematically and to look deeply into that third dimension. Only then can we begin to feel truly confident that we have our environment under control.

Limit Your Scope, Scan by Grid

One of the best ways to learn how to look is to hunt. When I'm in the backcountry hunting elk with friends like Andy Stumpf and Evan Hafer (two brilliant hunters), surrounded by hundreds of thousands of acres of wilderness, searching for creatures who have evolved over hundreds of thousands of years to blend into their environment, simply scanning my surroundings isn't going to get me anywhere. I have to look deeply and systematically to find the elk.

To do that, I do pretty much exactly what I used to do as a sniper with the *Commanders In-extremis* Force. I set up in a protected, low-visibility position with my rifle. I pick out an area in front of me to examine. I look at that piece of ground through my spotting scope and break it down into a grid (2x2, 3x3, 4x4—whatever works for you, though I wouldn't go much smaller). Then, I begin scanning—left to right, then right to left, from the bottom up—so my eyes never break contact with the piece of ground.

With each grid section I look as deeply as I can into that space, tracing through the image in a snake pattern. I'm looking for an elk, of course, but absent one, I'm looking for indications that an elk might have been there or might come through there at some point. I'm looking for signs in the brush—for anomalies in my mental picture, for spikes in the graph. In this case, that could mean foliage that has been disturbed where an elk may have bedded down. It could mean rut marks on the base of a tree. It could mean a thicket of berries that you know elk love to eat. Spikes like those are telling me, as a hunter, that something has been here, or is going to be here, and I need to pay attention to it if I want to accomplish my objective.

This is the same approach you can take to scanning your environment for threats. Every time you walk into a bar; whenever you go through an airport or board a plane; each new neighborhood or city or country you visit—wherever you go, scan the area segment by segment, left to right, right to left, bottom to top, looking for signs that something out of the ordinary is going on or is about to happen, something that you need to keep tabs on.

5s AND 25s

It's not enough, though, to survey only what is right in front of you—even if you're able to look deeply into that space. You have to expand your sphere of observation beyond what you can see at first glance, to look for possible threats that might be looming in the distance. In Iraq and Afghanistan, this is something we did as a matter of standard operating procedure every time we hit an IED or we had to stop our patrol (for any reason and for any length of time).

It's a security protocol that we call "5s and 25s." The moment we stop, every person in the patrol scans a five-meter radius around their position, ideally without yet exiting the vehicle. Once that area is cleared, we push out to twenty-five meters, scanning the whole way. The logic is straightforward. It's based on experience, on millions of miles driven by American military personnel during Operation Enduring Freedom (OEF) and Operation Iraqi Freedom (OIF): if there's one bomb, there are probably two bombs.

Secondary Attacks

Secondary attacks are a major issue, not just on the battlefield but also in active shooter and terrorism situations. During the Route 91 Harvest country music festival massacre in Las Vegas in 2017, after the first volleys of fire from the thirty-second floor of the Mandalay Bay hotel, the shooter attempted to blow up a jet fuel tank that sat along the perimeter of the tarmac at the Las Vegas Airport about six hundred yards from the festival grounds. His goal, after chaos broke out, was to create a secondary explosion to send concertgoers fleeing in the other direction, funneling them into what was effectively a kill zone. He was unsuccessful (jet fuel is not easily combustible), but in the years after, that moment inspired a good amount of rethinking and training by law enforcement and first responder agencies to account for secondary attacks when doing triage, establishing hot and cold zones, and setting up security perimeters during active shooter and terror events.

The goal of 5s and 25s is simple. In the event of an IED detonation, we're trying to prevent a second explosion, put ourselves in a position to effectively repel any secondary attack, and evacuate our wounded and KIA. In the event of a patrol stoppage, the goal is to set up a perimeter with a sizable enough area for us to more easily address whatever it is that got us to stop in the first place— in many cases that still means scanning for IEDs. Regardless, the overarching goal is always safety and security. It's risk mitigation and threat reduction through a simple set of key words that focus our attention on the specific task of deliberate observation.

In the Marine Corps's Field Service Medical Officer (FSMO) course, there is a large block of instruction on IEDs that includes a list of possible roadside IED indicators. Here are just a few of them:

Unusual behavior patterns or changes in community patterns, such as noticeably fewer people or vehicles in a normally busy area, open windows, or the absence of women or children.

People videotaping ordinary activities or military actions.

Suspicious objects.

New or out-of-place objects in an environment, such as dirt piles, construction, dead animals, or trash.

Signs that are newly erected or seem out of place. Obstacles in the roadway to channel traffic.

They're basically describing spikes in the pattern. Or as the Marine Corps puts it in the training materials, "The primary indication of an IED will be a *change in the baseline* . . ." But not just of the ground right in front of your face, also in the concentric circles out to twenty-five meters or more.

We can use this same set of tactics to expand our situational awareness in uncertain dynamic environments and increase our survivability in the process. We could be deep in the backcountry hunting elk and stumble into bear territory. We could be driving through Tornado Alley in late spring and be headed straight toward a developing storm cell. We could be at an outdoor music festival. We could be at a Black Friday sale in one of those massive big box stores. We could be unintentionally approaching a violent protest on our daily commute. We could be somewhere new and unfamiliar. In each of these scenarios—and an infinite number of others—being able to systematically scan our immediate surroundings and then extend our observation outward beyond our normal field of vision doesn't just give us the maximum amount of information to make a good decision, it gives us the time and distance necessary to execute on that decision successfully.

THE PEOPLE

Spikes in the pattern of your environment are a good indicator that threats may be present. But it's people, most often, who represent the actual threats. When you take a second look at the entire list of potential IED indicators enumerated in the Marines' FSMO course instruction, what you notice is that just as frequently as they mention things that stand out, they mention *people* that stand out. People in places they normally wouldn't be. People not in places they normally would be. People doing things that no one else is doing. People not doing things that everyone else is doing.

These are universal threat indicators. They are not just relevant to IEDs or to combat. In 2022, during the first round of the NBA playoffs, the animal rights group Direct Action Everywhere (DxE) organized a coordinated protest against Glen Taylor, the owner of the Minnesota Timberwolves (he owns a poultry business). On two separate occasions, DxE activists rushed the court during a Timberwolves home game—one tried to glue herself to the court, the other chained herself to the basket and tossed flyers into the stands. Then at the start of the third quarter of Game 4 against the Memphis Grizzlies, two women snuck down to seats in the second row right behind the Timberwolves' bench and Taylor's seats. One of the women used her phone to film the protest, and the other waited for the perfect moment to leap out of the crowd. Her goal, according to a DxE spokesperson afterward, was to whistle the owner for a "technical foul" and "eject" him from the game (the woman was wearing a referee shirt under her jacket).

The footage, captured by the television broadcast cameras, is amazingly instructive. Everything about these two women spiked the pattern. The behavior of the protesters was clearly an anomaly from the baseline of an NBA playoff game. These obviously weren't their seats (seats along the court are often empty right after halftime). They weren't cheering. They weren't following the flow of game action. And when her compatriot was about to make her move, the woman filming held her phone discreetly at chest level in landscape mode. All very weird.

Someone else noticed this, too: the security guard seated at the end of their row. She had one eye on them and one eye on the floor (broadcast footage caught this as well). When the moment came, the protester didn't even make it past the sideline in front of the courtside seats. The security guard leaped over the seats and pancake tackled her to the floor. She'd clocked the spikes in the pattern from these activists, she was vigilant, and when the threat materialized, she acted decisively.

But you don't have to be a trained security professional to possess the conscious observation skills necessary to defuse an incident or protect yourself from a situation like this one. You just have to know what to look for, *who* to look for, and where to look.

Hands, Demeanor

In his advanced situational awareness training classes, Yousef Badou teaches students how to identify threats through visible biometric indicators: flushed or pale skin; shallow, fast breathing; elevated heart rate; sweating; fidgeting. These involuntary functions are spikes in the normal behavior pattern, typically triggered by the adrenaline and cortisol coursing through the system of someone about to do some sketchy stuff, someone who is nervous or scared or excited. These signals are not to be dismissed. Yet interestingly, they were not what the security guard at the Minnesota Timberwolves game keyed on. She homed in on the protesters' hands and demeanor.

This wasn't by chance. She didn't just get lucky. She understood that a person's hands and their demeanor are the two most consistent and most important threat indicators. A person's demeanor is going to be the thing that most quickly spikes the pattern, and their hands are where the threat is most likely to materialize from—whether it's a gun or a knife, whether they try to snatch your purse or your child or grab your attention with a protest at a basketball game. It's the hands that do the dirty work.

Hands and demeanor don't just show you whether someone is a threat, they also show you whether someone is vulnerable. In October 2021, three teenage males attempted to rob a gas station in Yuma, Arizona. Dressed in jeans and black hoodies with their faces obscured, they entered through the front double doors of the station's convenience store. The male in front raised a pistol, announcing their intentions, and the second male filed in right behind him.

The first person the assailants encountered was a customer who just happened to be a former Marine. When he heard the men enter, the veteran turned to find a pistol pointed in his direction and an attacker in a very vulnerable posture. He only had one hand on his weapon, and the other was holding his waistband like a "badass." His feet were close together and he was back on his heels with no forward momentum. He was clearly unsure or nervous about how to commit this robbery.

The former Marine clocked all this in the first two seconds after the first guy walked through the door, and he responded. With one hand, the Marine reached for the assailant's shooting hand and thrust it upward, immediately knocking him off balance. At the same time, he closed the distance and, with momentum and gravity on his side, easily took the young man to the ground. As that happened, the two accomplices immediately fled, one of whom hadn't even had a chance to get through the doors.

In this case, the teenage male's hands and demeanor showed that he was a threat to the safety of everyone in the gas station convenience store, and that he was vulnerable to anyone with good situational awareness, a resilient mindset, and sufficient training.

Putting It All Together

In simplest terms, your situational awareness and the prospect of your safety are determined by how well you combine surveillance of your immediate surroundings with a scan of the people in that environment. To limit the cognitive load of doing unique, location-specific deep surveillance every time you enter a new space, there's a simple approach you can use that works for 99 percent of situations.

Every time you enter a new, unfamiliar, uncomfortable, or potentially dangerous space—let's use a restaurant in a suburban mall as an example here—first get your bearings in the environment. Where are the exits? What is the most direct path to those exits? Does the place look clean? Do the tables and chairs look like they're in good condition? Does the place *feel* safe?

Next, quickly scan from left to right to get a sense for how many people are in the room and if anything immediately jumps out. It's a mall, so most likely the tables are full of couples, friends, and families. If you spot a table where someone is eating alone, maybe you zero in on that person first. You might notice that he's not distracted by people or his phone; he's alert and aware of his surroundings. You catch him scanning the hands and demeanor of other patrons, and you realize he's doing everything you're doing.

As Yousef Badou would advise, you won't know if he's a good guy or a bad guy unless things pop off, but you'll want to know where he is if and when they do. Either you will need to neutralize or escape from him, or you will want to team up with him as a way to increase your chances of survival. It's always good to watch the watchers.

Training Hands, Demeanor

Following the full "hands, demeanor" protocol every time you enter a room is obviously impractical. Not only does it take too much time and energy, but you'll look like a weirdo and unnerve your family—and their calm, comfort, and safety is the whole reason you're working on your situational awareness and cultivating this level of preparedness. That said, it's important to practice systematically scanning the ground in front of you and the people around you. So, take one day every week to fully engage your senses and scan everywhere you go. The goal is not just to develop proficiency, but to build a new habit that becomes automatic and efficient and unobtrusive as a result. Basically, be aware without fully being aware that you're being aware! Easier said than done, but necessary in your journey toward being prepared.

If you don't see any solo diners who spike the pattern, scan left to right again, this time more methodically, looking at the hands of anyone who seems like they could have the capacity to be a threat, then up to their faces to see if their demeanor matches what their hands are doing.

Are they engrossed in their phones? Are they leaning back in their chairs, smiling, enjoying conversation? Are they pushed into the table eating their food? All these are normal baseline patterns for a busy mall restaurant.

Then what about that couple over on the right side of the dining room? The girlfriend is leaning back in her chair with her arms folded. The boyfriend is leaning forward aggressively. His face is red, his neck muscles are tense, and he's whisper-yelling. It's very obvious they're in an argument.

But where are his hands? Are they wildly gesticulating? Is he periodically pounding the table in frustration? While these are aggressive postures, they are relatively normal for a fight between romantic partners. However, if his hands are inside his jacket, if he's reaching into a bag, if he's jabbing his finger in her face . . . those are spikes in the pattern. Maybe it's nothing, maybe it's something. Either way, it's definitely something you need to pay attention to and be ready to do something about.

Ask the host to seat you on the side of the restaurant opposite the couple, ideally close to an exit (front or back). Make sure you're seated with a view of the couple and have as many paths of egress as possible. And if things don't calm down, if you and your family continue to feel uncomfortable, prepare to act. Ask that the couple be removed; move to a table farther away; get up and leave; or if things start to escalate . . . intervene.

These are all viable options. Which one is best will be context dependent and entirely up to you. But make no mistake, you *will* have to pick one.

DENIAL IS THE BIGGEST THREAT

Whether or not to take action in the face of imminent danger might seem like a no-brainer. It would certainly seem like the single most important factor in determining your survival in a catastrophe. But the reality is, the bigger issue is whether or not you even accept the presence of imminent danger at all.

It sounds absurd that when faced with a grievous threat to your safety you might deny its existence. Except, almost everyone does it. It's practically a cultural script. We hear a window shatter downstairs in the middle of the night. We feel the ground violently shake and see the chandelier swinging wildly from the ceiling. We hear gunshots ring out from the office down the hall. And what's the first thing we do when something like that spikes the pattern? We come up with some ridiculous explanation for it that dismisses any possibility of true danger.

It's not an intruder breaking a window; it's probably the cat knocking a glass off the counter. But your cat died eight years ago, and now you have a dog, who is asleep at the foot of the bed.

It's not a large earthquake; it's probably just the garbage truck. But it's Tuesday, and garbage day is Thursday.

It's not gunfire; it's probably just construction noise, or a movie playing too loudly, or a car backfiring. But cars don't backfire three times per second. Indeed, in the aftermath of nearly every school shooting in America, you will find a news clip of a teacher describing the initial moments of chaos, unsure of what was happening until they heard the screaming of children.

These periods of disbelief between a spike in the pattern and recognition (and acceptance) of the danger are typically brief, but they are still long enough in many cases to be the difference between life and death.

In 2004, a 9.1 magnitude earthquake struck in the Indian Ocean, just off the northern coast of the island of Sumatra in Indonesia. The quake produced a series of massive tsunami waves that raced across the Indian Ocean in all directions and ultimately killed 230,000 people in fourteen countries. One of the first places the tsunami made landfall was the island of Phuket, the popular Thailand tourist destination four hundred kilometers east across the Andaman Sea. Before the first waves arrived, though, a ten-year-old English girl named Tilly Smith was walking along Mai Khao beach with her family when she noticed the sea receding from the shoreline and the water frothing weirdly on the surface. Two weeks earlier Tilly had learned about tsunamis in her geography class, and now everything she was seeing out beyond the shore screamed tsunami to her. There was only one problem: nobody would listen to her.

"My mum didn't believe me. She didn't react and just kept on walking," Tilly told reporters afterward. "I was screaming, 'Please Mum, please come back with me . . . If you don't . . . you won't survive.'"

Finally, her father started to worry about the level of panic

Tilly was displaying and the fact that she couldn't be consoled. He took her to the security staff at the resort where they were vacationing so she could explain to them what she knew was looming, quite literally, out on the horizon. Thankfully, the staff had been taking in news reports of the magnitude of the earthquake, and everything Tilly was describing to them made sense, so they immediately evacuated the beach.

Just in time.

Mai Khao beach would be the only place on the entire island of Phuket that reported no casualties. By being aware of her environment, spotting the spike in the pattern, and acting decisively, officials estimate that Tilly—a ten-year-old girl on Christmas vacation—saved at least a hundred lives.

Just imagine if she'd listened to her mother, or if her father had been able to calm her down and they didn't go report what she was seeing to the resort staff. Imagine the death toll.

It's not hard to imagine when you consider the capacity of a typical adult to deny the presence of imminent danger even as it crashes through your kitchen window, kicks down your front door, and races toward your shores. The capacity seems almost endless, for two main reasons.

One is a lack of exposure to certain kinds of danger: violence, firearms, natural disasters, wild animals, et cetera. We don't have experience with the type of stress these things produce, so we lack the specific kind of resilience and awareness necessary to recognize the threat right away and to act in our own defense in a timely manner.

The other reason is that, as a culture, we have become soft and lazy. We don't just want to be comfortable all the time, we *demand* comfort—from our cars, our theater seats, our apartments, our clothes—and we don't like to think about that comfort being violated. This includes contemplating death, which we insulate ourselves from as much as possible, both with our choices and our thoughts. *I'm a safe, good, conscientious person,* we tell ourselves, *so bad things shouldn't happen to me. Bad stuff only happens to other people . . . bad people.* It's not that we believe we're immortal or invincible when those subconscious thoughts influence our relationship to preparedness; it's just that deep down we believe we're going to die the "normal way"—when we're old, in our bed, when we're ready, when we've decided it's time to go. (As if we have any control over that whatsoever.) And so, when bad shit finally does find us, we deny its existence at first, because we refuse to believe these things happen to people like us. We don't accept that it's our time, that it's our turn, to our ultimate detriment.

You can do everything right in the realm of preparedness, but if you indulge the kind of arrogant delusion that convinces you that bad stuff like a tsunami on your vacation couldn't possibly be happening, then you are in danger. (And so might the lives of hundreds of other people.) If you refuse to see what's right in front of you, because it's too scary to contemplate, you are as good as helpless.

You might think you will know what's coming. You might

think you have a good feel for your surroundings and a solid grasp on the people in your midst, but you won't. *You can't.* Denial will have prevented you from really knowing how to *look*, and any hope for robust situational awareness will be forever out of your grasp.

4

DECISION POINT

What are you going to do?

That is *the* question. Everything up to this point has been about preparing you for the moment when you have to answer it.

Forging resilience. Making plans. Building situational awareness. These are mental tools designed to cultivate quick decision-making and help you to take the correct actions when catastrophe strikes—when that thing you are most terrified of, that has brought you on this journey to preparedness, has come to pass. Because when your worst nightmare has been made real, and you need to fight or flee to survive, stress will be high, and time will be short.

You won't have the luxury of contemplation, of second-guessing, of "wait and see." You'll have to act—to go, to move, to hide, to shoot, to kill if that's what it takes to keep you and your loved ones safe.

Now.

This idea that you'll have to think quickly and make snap decisions in an emergency probably doesn't sound revolutionary. You're probably thinking, *Yeah, no shit, Mike.* Except it's never that simple. Most people struggle with decision-making. All of the popular training and books on decision-making are aimed at leaders—in business, in politics, in the military. It's the same in every case. There is rarely anything for the average person, the normal mom and dad. As a result, there are a discouragingly large number of people out there who aren't comfortable with making important decisions. They try to avoid having to make them, or they defer to others, constantly concerned about making the wrong choice.

This kind of attitude puts you at a distinct disadvantage when it comes to catastrophe, because it produces a potentially deadly delay in response time. This delay is not the same kind of shutdown as a parasympathetic response. It's more like analysis paralysis. You're not frozen in fear. You're stuck in place by indecision. The perception of having too many options makes quick decision-making a near impossible task.

The way through this mental block is to do two things: recognize that you're already good at decision-making, and focus on making your decisions under stress as simple as possible.

EVERYTHING IS A BUNCH OF DECISIONS

One of the smartest people I know on the topic of decision-making is a former Army Ranger and Special Missions Unit operator named Tom Flanagan. Like many of the special operations folks who were in the military during those first handful of years after 9/11, Tom saw serious combat where little decisions had big impacts. He was in it, constantly. He was also one of those guys who seemed to be good at everything he touched.

But it wasn't always that way for him, as he'll happily tell you. During his first two years as a wrestler in high school, for example, he was terrible. He had a significant losing record. He trained as hard as he could, but it didn't change the results. He kept getting caught and outpointed. He kept losing. Then one weekend he ran into a state champion wrestler at a meet and asked him a very basic question that produced a very powerful answer.

"How are you so good?" Tom asked him. "What made you so good at what you're doing?"

"Wrestling," the champion told him, "is a bunch of decisions, back to back to back. You try one move, and it doesn't work, so you go to the next one, and the next one, and the next one."

It was a process, Tom realized, one that involves a lot of trial and error. But if one wants to be great, it requires nothing more than consistently "making the right decisions in order," as he puts it. Tom threw himself into this process, and by the time he finished his senior year, he could confidently put a dozen or more good decisions together on the mat, in the form of moves and countermoves, very quickly. The result was an incredible record in his last wrestling season and an overall winning record for his entire high school career.

Tom went from losing to winning on the back of this simple piece of advice, and he carried it with him into the army, and into a successful career in special operations and combat. We can also learn to carry it into preparedness. Survival in a catastrophe is all about making as many correct decisions in a row as possible, as quickly as possible, while being able to move seamlessly to the next best option when our first choice doesn't work.

That can sound intimidating, like there's choreography that you have to learn ahead of time, but we already do a version of this every day in nearly every aspect of our lives. At home with our kids, in the car driving, in the office at work, at a bar in conversation, in the gym going through a workout, in the wilderness hiking toward a camping spot. Everything you do in these scenarios is a series of decisions, one right after the other. Some of them you do out of habit in a string of perfect choices (your morning routine, for instance); others are maybe more difficult and variable and include some wrong turns that require pivots to get where you want to go (like getting your kids dressed and fed).

That they maybe don't *feel* like decisions to you, or that you feel like you take these actions unconsciously, is beside the point. It doesn't change the fact that they are decisions made by the conscious mind. And if anything, you should take some comfort in knowing that, unwittingly, you're pretty damn good at them.

You're here, aren't you? You're alive. You've managed to navigate and survive the chaos and uncertainty of modern life. What this should tell you is that you have good muscle memory and solid instincts. Without actively thinking about it, you make enough right decisions during the course of the day to get the kids off to school, to get to work unscathed, to get through conversations and workouts and hikes through the backcountry without getting your ass handed to you.

To put it plainly, you know how to make decisions. Your muscle memory is just the brain's way of encoding the most efficient decisions in everyday scenarios into what feels like your unconscious behavior. Your instincts aren't some weird set of gut impulses that exist separately from your mind. They're simply another way to describe what you intuitively know are the best decisions in life-threatening situations. They're telling you that *you already know how to survive.*

Being properly prepared is just making the conscious decision, ahead of time, to be more aware of that muscle memory and be better connected to those instincts, because they need to be right there at your fingertips to drive quick decision-making when it matters most. When the bullets are flying or the fire is raging, there is no time for deep thinking and higher-order executive functions. That work needs to be done and trained for as part of your planning so that you can shut out the noise, shed all the bullshit, and listen only for that knowing voice when everything is on the line.

GET OFF THE X

The first thing that voice in your head is most likely to tell you is "Go!"

There is always a scene in a movie like *John Wick* where the main character is surrounded by bad guys and he visualizes the complete sequence of decisions he has to make to neutralize each of the attackers and escape. Then, he actually does it as scripted in his mind. It's awesome to watch. It's also fantasy.

More realistic are those scenes in movies like *The Bourne Identity* and shows like *The Terminal List*, where the main character relies on situational awareness to sense that danger's close and then decides very quickly to relocate. It's always a simple line like "We've got to move" or "We can't stay here."

I had my own version of that in my first combat experience in Afghanistan. As the rockets came flying into the landing zone for our water resupply, the first thing I did once I snapped back into the fight was to get everyone the hell off the HLZ. Before I hopped on the ATV and ripped a hole in the concertina wire, before I scanned the hillside for the source of the rockets, before I helped teammates set up defensive positions, I told everyone within earshot to move, move, move! I didn't tell them where to move, or for how long, or what to bring with them. I kept it simple and direct and immediate.

In special operations, we have a term for this first, quick decision in situations where you're on the back foot and being forced to react to your adversary's actions. It's called "getting off the X." Before you do anything, before you activate the first steps of your PACE plan (or better yet, *as* you activate them), you've got to get yourself out of the crosshairs and away from the current danger as best you can. This is as much for your immediate survival, as Tom Flanagan experienced in Iraq, as it is for flipping the playing field.

As the sun came up early one morning in October 2005, Tom and members of his unit found themselves in the crosshairs of what felt like an entire army of Iraqi insurgents. Set up in a house off a dirt road in a rural part of the country, Tom and his team woke up that morning to a deafening barrage of enemy gunfire coming in from all directions. "Small-arms fire, machine-gun rounds, RPGs, you name it, it came flying through every window, through every wooden door, through every wall right into the house," Tom described to me. "I was sure at that moment that this was it. We weren't coming home from this." Everyone on the team knew right away that if they wanted to prevent that worst-case scenario from happening, they all needed to start making some decisions.

"You didn't really hear any chatter over the radio. We all just knew our individual decisions from that point forward would greatly affect the outcome of the fight," Tom recalled.

Immediately, everyone started to move, posting up in the nearest protected location to return fire. Everyone except Tom, who was in the middle of the house and effectively pinned down by the incoming rounds crisscrossing in every direction. For a few moments—a minute, maybe less—Tom had a 360-degree view of his guys. "As I looked around the house," he said, "I saw some of the most extraordinary acts of heroism I'd ever seen in combat," including one guy shooting 203 rounds (the ammunition for a grenade launcher) into a brick wall fifteen feet directly in front of him, with no concern for the shrapnel and debris kicking back in his direction, to create a hole that would provide more direct access for him and his teammates to fire on the enemy.

This gave Tom a chance to move. With bullets flying everywhere, the only direction he could move was up, so he ran up to the roof. From that elevated position, Tom was able to engage directly with combatants who were in fixed positions, then suppress any vehicle convoys trying to approach. He was also able to spot a mortar position about a mile from their location and task an unmanned aerial vehicle (or UAV) to take it out.

Eventually, Tom and his team got off the back foot and turned the tide, inflicting numerous casualties and massive damage to the enemy's ability to fight, all without sustaining a single casualty themselves. "Not even a graze from a passing bullet," Tom recounted, still amazed to this day. Make no mistake: all of their success, every decisive moment in the battle, began with their initial decision to get off the X and move.

If you are one of those people who struggles with decision-making, who is terrified of not knowing what to do in an emergency, make this your automatic first decision: get off the X. Aside from its obvious survival value, like we just illustrated, it also has the added double benefit of honing down subsequent choices while building decision-making momentum.

Okay, we're moving. Now what? I do this or I do that. I go here or I go there.

That's how your brain will start to orient itself in a crisis. By making that first decision, you remove a whole mess of options that were still viable when the slate was blank but now no longer make sense. What's left are fewer, more obvious, and directly impactful choices, which results in much easier, quicker decision-making. Even more, when you take this approach you are also fighting off the chance of parasympathetic shutdown and naturally preempting all the higher-order thinking that can produce analysis paralysis.

In Michael Lewis's book *The Premonition*, you meet a former ICU doctor named Carter Mecher, who was an expert in medical error, who ran the VA hospital in Chicago, and who became responsible for crafting most of America's pandemic policy prior to COVID-19. He tells the story of a group of soldiers lost in the Alps who find a map in one of their backpacks and follow it to safety, only to realize later that the map was for the Pyrenees, eight hundred miles southwest of the Alps. It had nothing to do with the Alps, at all. Mecher was making a point about the power of maps and planning to just get you moving. "A map has value when you're lost," he said, "because it gives you a starting point." Mecher took a similar approach into the ICU with patients on the brink of death and doctors on the verge of panic. Because that's what happens, he described, if doctors don't know what to do or where to start or they feel like the patient is out of options: they panic, they don't do anything, and the patients die. "Having something in front of you" to get you started, Mecher said, "even if it isn't completely right, is better than nothing."

At the head of your PACE plan, at the top of your decision tree, foremost in your mind as you scan the hands and demeanor of people in a sketchy environment, should be this first decision that you must always be ready to make: get off the X.

ARE YOU READY FOR DEADLY FORCE?

The most important lifesaving decision you might ever have to make involves, paradoxically, whether to take a life. In the decision-making matrix of survival in chaos, this decision typically comes later. How much later depends entirely on your level of mental preparedness around the topic of deadly force because that decision point only comes when you believe events are about to catastrophically cascade and you have reached a point of no return.

Over the course of my post-military career teaching self-protection as part of preparedness, I have come to realize that virtually no one puts enough thought into their personal criteria for using deadly force. When I ask people who think they know what theirs are to describe them for me, inevitably they start rattling off a bunch of legal jargon, or they describe a scenario from an episode of *Law & Order*, or they recite something about the so-called castle doctrine and stand-your-ground laws that they heard on a talk radio show.

What these people are doing is not describing the circumstances in which they would feel morally justified using deadly force in defense of themselves or others; they're giving me the legal rationale for why they won't go to jail for it. They're arguing to me why no one has the right to judge them for their actions when they're being threatened and have done nothing to deserve it. Except I wasn't asking them to explain how or when they might be able to use legally justifiable deadly force. This says to me that none of these folks had any real idea which ethical or circumstantial boxes they needed to have checked *for themselves* before they felt okay pulling the trigger.

Does the assailant need to be armed? Does it matter if the kids aren't home or in the car, and it's just you two? If they're trying to rob you, does it matter what they are trying to take? Does the attacker have to be bigger than you? Do you need to be trapped? If it's clear they're on drugs, does that change the calculation? Is the fact that they've broken into your home all you need? Do you need to be in fear for your life? Does their gun need to be pointed at your head, or is it being in their hand enough provocation for you? What if you're really scared but the intruder says repeatedly that they're not going to hurt you—does that matter?

When I ask these questions, most people can't help getting flustered. They feel like they're being unfairly judged, and they can't help responding from a place of strong emotions. But unchecked emotions are exactly the problem. They are what will get you killed or thrown in jail.

In his book *When Violence Is the Answer*, the self-protection specialist Tim Larkin describes two kinds of violence: social aggression and asocial violence. Social aggression is the kind of violence, he says, that involves talking. It's the loud threats, the posturing, and shit-talking at the bar—the harassing behavior. Asocial violence is the kind where there are no words being spoken. Where nothing you can say will elicit a response from the attacker or stop their attack. Asocial violence is psychopathic Terminator mode—that person is there to do you harm, no two ways about it.

Larkin's argument is that ninety-nine times out of a hundred, what you deal with out in the world is antisocial violence, which is scary and dangerous, but also avoidable. You can talk your way out of it, you can run away, you can deescalate, or you can make a show of force that neutralizes the threat. But that one time when it's asocial violence, when the time for words has gone, there is no escaping the fact that you will have to use violence to protect yourself and potentially save others.

The decorated former Navy SEAL Jocko Willink has talked about this same idea in the context of jiujitsu training for self-defense. If you square up on him, push him, try to punch or kick him, start yelling that you want to fight him, he says, "Guess what I'm going to do? I'm going to run away. I don't want to get involved. I don't want to fight you. You could stab me. You could sue me after I get done throwing you down on the concrete. A million bad things could happen, and almost none of them are good." Where this all changes, he says, "is when you grab me. Now I don't have the option to run away. I have to know how to get away." His choices at that point have evaporated, and the situation has gone from antisocial to asocial, and now he has to act.

That's probably the best way to think about using deadly force in a life-or-death situation. If you can avoid it, you should do everything in your power to avoid it. You should use your feet as your first line of self-defense, as Jocko put it. If you can't do that, then you should know how to use deadly force and be prepared to use it without hesitation. (Which means training in something like jiujitsu or wrestling or boxing, as well as getting proper equipment and training with firearms, which we'll talk about in the next chapter.)

There are two reasons that taking this kind of care and consideration with deadly force is so important: the legal and the moral ramifications. If someone breaks into your home or carjacks you with a gun, in most American jurisdictions you will be within your legal rights to use deadly force to protect yourself. That *does not mean* you will be free of the legal system, however. As the authorities do their duty and make sure that your actions were within the law, you'll be talking to the police a lot. There's a chance the family of the deceased will sue for wrongful death. There's a chance the local district attorney will consider bringing charges against you. Even if they're lesser, misdemeanor charges, that still means you will have to hire an attorney. If the media gets a hold of your story, then you'll have to deal with their questions and the potential that everyone in your town is going to know your business. It's all much more complicated than just what the letter of the law allows for.

The moral ramifications are much simpler. If you use deadly force, you will have to live the rest of your life knowing that you took a life. Whether it was legally justified or not, knowing that you are responsible for another human being no longer being on this earth is a very heavy thing. All of us in the military and law enforcement community made that bargain going in, and still some of us struggle with the lives we've taken because we hadn't yet figured out the personal criteria that made use of deadly force morally justifiable *to ourselves.*

For a civilian, for a normal mom and dad, the decision to take a life in self-defense can happen in the blink of an eye, but the emotional and spiritual consequences can last for the rest of their lives. I want you to be able to live with the life-or-death decisions you make under stress, so this is something you have to think about beforehand. It's something you have to plan and train for. Most importantly, it's something you will need to have decided in advance, before you find yourself in the middle of the worst day of your life.

To help people figure out their personal criteria and find their line in the sand, I run a scared-straight type scenario during self-protection classes. It tends to shake people up, but it also reassures them because what they realize by the end is that almost no one is on the same page as it relates to the use of deadly force. Everyone is struggling to figure out how they really feel about deadly force and what they'd actually do when push came to shove.

The exercise usually plays out something like this:

I select a diverse cross-section of people from the class and ask them to stand up in front of the room and close their eyes. I tell them that I'm about to walk them through a home invasion scenario, and I instruct them that at the point in the scenario when they believe they would use deadly force, they should turn around and sit on the floor, as a gesture of full commitment to their choice. When it's clear everyone understands the rules, I begin.

"It's late," I say. "Close to midnight. It's late spring, early summer. It's hot. The air conditioner is cranking. Your spouse is out of town on a work trip. Your kids, ages nine and thirteen, are asleep in their bedrooms down the hall. You hear a noise that you recognize as the sound of your front door opening.

You get out of bed, grab your pistol from the lockbox on your nightstand, and you go investigate. As you come out into the living room with your pistol held out in front of you, in the direction of the noise, you see the shadowy figure of a man crossing from the front door to the other side of the living room. As your eyes adjust to the darkness, you see what looks like a gun in the figure's hand."

Immediately, several people turn around and sit down.

"The figure crosses the living room," I continue to describe to the group. "He's moving toward the hallway where your kids' rooms are."

More people turn and sit.

"He walks down the hall and stops at the door of your thirteen-year-old son's room and turns the handle."

More people turn and sit. There are times when everyone in the exercise will have sat down by this point, but quite often there is a surprising number of people still standing, so I continue.

"The figure raises the gun and enters the room, closing the door behind them. You chase after the person and open your son's door to find the figure standing over your son, bending down with the gun in his hand."

This is usually when the last of the people finally turn and sit, but if there's one or two left, I continue.

"You turn on the light. It's your son's friend who lives across the street. His family is going on vacation the next day, and he just wanted to return the NERF gun that he'd borrowed from your son the other day. The boy is crying now because he's got a pistol pointed at his head, and the crying wakes up your son. Just then, amid the confusion, you hear the bedroom door open. You turn, and in the dark hallway you see the outline of a large figure and the muzzle of a shotgun. Then a bright light flashes in your eyes."

The last person turns and sits.

"It was a sheriff's deputy. They'd received a report of a suspicious figure sneaking across the lawn of this address and entering the home. You've just killed a law enforcement officer," I tell them. End of scenario.

Now here's the thing: at no point did any one of the volunteers in the exercise make a calculated decision based on criteria they'd established for themselves ahead of time about the use of deadly force. They all had their own reasons for turning around and sitting down when they did, but none of them were acting on a set of circumstantial parameters that they'd arrived at in advance. They were reacting to the heightened emotional tenor of the situation. They were acting out of fear and panic. They were responding automatically to their unconscious trauma triggers. They were operating from a place of incomplete knowledge—the cortisol and adrenaline pumping through their system wasn't allowing them to take in all the information and process it, so they were only getting slivers of the whole picture, like looking at black-and-white snapshots in an old View-Master.

So how do you avoid finding yourself in a potentially regrettable situation like this? First, like I've talked about, you need to decide *ahead of time* what conditions need to be present for the use of deadly force to be morally justifiable to yourself. Second, you need to assert yourself in the situation early and try to mitigate any potential escalation of force.

Tim Larkin and Jocko Willink would say that 99 percent of violent encounters are antisocial or avoidable. I tend to agree. In this home invasion scenario, instead of staying quiet like a church mouse for fear of being spotted, or hoping the intruder just goes away, or waiting for an opportunity to shoot, announce yourself. Flip on the lights. Positively identify the intruder with your pistol presented, and then use firm verbal commands to disarm them. "Don't move or I'll shoot you in your fucking face!" "Drop the gun and get on the ground right now or I will fire on you!" You can de-escalate and neutralize a potentially violent situation with your words by moving first and flipping the dynamic with your own threat of violence. Just because you're trained to use deadly force and you're prepared to use it doesn't mean you *have to* . . . until you absolutely do.

The famed Austrian psychologist Viktor Frankl once wrote, "Between stimulus and response there is a space. In that space is our power to choose our response." In catastrophe, in times of maximum stress where the stakes are as high as they'll ever be, no two spaces are more important than the ones we fill with our first and last choices. Our decision whether to get off the X at the first sign of danger and our decision whether to shoot in self-defense as a last resort—these are the decisions we have to be prepared to make at a moment's notice. We cannot be scared to make them. Because "in our response," Viktor Frankl continued, "lies our growth and our freedom."

Also in our response, I would argue, lies our survival.

Decision-making is an essential skill for preparedness. This includes making decisions quickly, making them correctly, making adjustments when they are wrong, making sure you know what you will do before you ever need to do it, and making peace with yourself when you have to make the most difficult decision of them all. These are not easy. They won't be painless. You won't leave an encounter with a life-threatening catastrophe totally unscathed. But you can survive it. And that is the ultimate objective.

5

EVERYDAY CARRY (EDC)

As a Special Operations veteran in various US Army counterterrorism units, my understanding of everyday carry (or EDC) considerations was always defined from, and somewhat limited to, an operational requirement and risk mitigation perspective. I knew what to wear and what to bring on every mission to achieve its objectives and increase the chances of returning to base in one piece. If we were operating offensively at night, going after bad guys or doing direct-action raids of hard targets, I knew I would need a specific EDC: zip ties, ammo, flash-bangs, night vision goggles, grenades, spare batteries for my optics, tourniquet, among other things.

It wasn't until I left the military and joined the Central Intelligence Agency as a Global Response Staff (GRS) officer that I learned how extensive and ever-present your everyday carry considerations could and should be. My first glimpse into this new understanding came during a rotation in a beautiful desert vacation destination known as [redacted]. I was off duty, walking around the base in a pair of flip-flops one afternoon, when my boss came over to me.

"Mike, don't wear those on the base," he said, gesturing down to my flip-flops.

I was confused. I knew the rules. I'd always followed proper army protocol wherever I was. "But I'm not working right now," I said.

"On this base, with only a handful of us here, you're always working," he said, "on duty or off." It clicked immediately and stayed with me long after I left the GRS and moved into preparedness training in the civilian world.

On that little base, out there in the middle of a twenty-first century Wild West, surrounded by hostiles, by desert, by the unknown, we were our own first responders. If shit went down, it wasn't going to be a quick-reaction force of the Seventy-Fifth Ranger Regiment that saved our ass. It was going to be the handful of guys on that base, which meant every one of us needed to be able to shoot, move, and communicate as quickly and effectively as possible if we wanted to survive. Every detail mattered. Everything we carried had a very specific and intentional purpose.

Have you ever tried to sprint in flip-flops? I have. It sucks, and it doesn't work. Have you ever tried to sprint in flip-flops, then navigate between obstacles, then stop on a dime, pivot, and return fire on enemy elements who got the jump on you? I haven't, thank God, because after that conversation I never wore flip-flops on a base again.

That's when I realized EDC isn't just the pistol in your waistband or the tourniquet in your pack; it's everything you are from head to toe. And it all matters.

YOU ARE ALWAYS YOUR OWN FIRST RESPONDER

In the military, we were never out on our own, flapping in the wind. We were always connected to support of some kind, whether it was a headquarters element monitoring our progress, close air support in the air above or offset nearby, or a quick-reaction force (QRF) ready to back us up if we got into trouble. We were always tethered to assets ready to support us in the worst-case scenario.

In the civilian world, we have a similar kind of support system. We have laws that tell us what is okay or not okay to do. We have signs that tell us where to go and how to get there. We have the fire department, the police department, and EMS to help us in an emergency; until we don't. And not just when society collapses in civil unrest or natural disaster strikes, but also when the numbers just aren't in our favor.

When I was out on missions as part of a twenty-four- to

thirty-six-man unit, those headquarters, air assets, and QRF elements were dedicated to *us* for the length of our mission. That's a hundred-plus people looking after us. Heber City, Utah, where my company is located, has only seventeen full-time police officers (with twelve to twenty reserve officers) dedicated to serving and protecting more than eighteen thousand people over a nine-square-mile area, *at all times*.

I talked about this in the chapter on planning—about how you need to have a plan for emergencies when the infrastructure collapses. But the world doesn't have to be falling apart for you to be in a life-or-death situation where you will have to handle yourself. In rural areas, on unincorporated land, in canyons and forests, official first-responder response times to distress calls can take twenty minutes or more on a good day. If you're out hiking and slip, break your femur, and slice your femoral artery, you can bleed out in as little as a few minutes unless you have what you need to stop the bleed. You could be hiking in the Hollywood Hills and you'd still be in trouble. EMS response times in populated areas range from seven to twelve minutes, on average. Double that in rural areas, with "nearly 1 of 10 encounters waiting almost a half hour for the arrival of EMS personnel," according to a 2017 study of nearly 1.8 million EMS calls.

The picture is even more dire when it comes to police response times. The average response time in the city of Los Angeles in 2021 was twenty minutes. It's ten minutes or longer in Atlanta, Denver, Detroit, and Houston. The Virginia Tech shooter fired 175 bullets and killed thirty people in that same amount of time. In Boston, Las Vegas, New York City, Washington DC, Seattle, Dallas, Miami, and Philadelphia, response times are anywhere from six to nine minutes. The shooting at Sandy Hook Elementary School in 2012 that took twenty innocent children from their families lasted five minutes. The 2015 shooting at the Emanuel AME Church in Charleston, South Carolina, lasted six minutes. The shooter was able to reload five times.

And then there is the flipside of that timeline, which we witnessed with the 2022 Uvalde, Texas, elementary school shooting where nineteen students and two teachers were killed, in no small part because it took officers an unbelievable, gut-wrenching seventy-four minutes and eight seconds to confront and kill the gunman.

None of this detail is to criticize the first responders in any of these cities—they have a difficult job in tough places, with budgets that are stretched thin and sometimes very poor leadership. Even under ideal conditions there's only so much they can do. Robberies and carjackings take less than a minute to transpire, for example. Only Superman is stopping those events before they happen. This illustrates that one of the factors that turns danger into catastrophe, that turns a day out in nature into the worst day of your life, is the extent to which you find yourself on your own, to figure out solutions and save yourself.

And this is where your EDC considerations come into play. Everyday carry is the foundation of the *physical* side of preparedness. You can have your spine stiffened and your head on a swivel, you can have a plan in place and be ready to go in an instant—*you can know what to do*—but if you don't have at least some of the physical items on your person that allow you to do what you need to do, for as long as you need to do it . . . then you're not prepared for anything.

THE ESSENTIALS OF EVERYDAY CARRY

The main goal at the heart of EDC strategy is to increase your capacity, which subsequently increases your capability, for self-defense and survival. Those ideas are related, but they are also distinct in that they require you to answer two separate questions as you think about your everyday carry.

How are you going to defend yourself or others against someone or something trying to harm you?

How are you going to treat yourself or others in the event of injury?

Self-Defense

There are two categories of self-defense items for everyday carry: lethal and nonlethal. Both are important to have. You want to be able to respond to threats with a corresponding or commensurate amount of force, but you also want to be able to extricate yourself from dangerous situations without using deadly force if you can. Like we talked about in the previous chapter, in situations where you feel like your life is in danger, the law is usually going to be on your side when it comes to the use of deadly force, assuming you have followed the law in that jurisdiction as it relates to concealed carry of deadly weapons. However, your life is still going to be legally and morally complicated for a while afterward, so if you can prevent that, you should. This is especially true if, in retrospect, you or the law think that *maybe* you could have protected yourself with a lesser degree of force. If only you had nonlethal options as part of your EDC.

Lethal Options

PISTOLS

As much as we would like to avoid the use of deadly force whenever possible, EDC for self-defense begins with concealed carry pistol considerations. If you are serious about being able to defend yourself and your family from imminent threats, you have to get serious about your choice of firearm.

Now, there is a school of thought in the self-defense world that puts the emphasis on the "concealed" part of concealed carry weapons. They advocate for the use of smaller pistols because they are low profile, low visibility. For women, experts in this school talk about little .22s that can fit in your purse. For men, they talk about .38s that can tuck into your beltline anywhere or into ankle holsters and fanny packs. They even have a name for these types of guns: pocket-ready pistols.

And while I agree that low profile and low visibility are absolute priorities when it comes to your EDC pistol, defaulting to smallness to achieve that is a big mistake for two reasons: capacity and capability. A smaller pistol typically means either fewer or smaller-caliber bullets—sometimes both. That translates to less stopping power and less capacity for defending yourself and those around you. This sounds obvious, and for the most part, it's undisputed. What is disputed by far too many people is whether it matters all that much, because they believe (or they hope) that the presence of the pistol alone will be a sufficient deterrent.

These are people who think that when they're accosted by a mugger or a rapist or an armed robber, if they pull out a pistol (of any kind) from their bag or their holster and aim it at their assailant, it will scare them off. And here's the thing: nine times out of ten, they're probably right. But that doesn't mean the strategy is right. It only takes one time being wrong to be dead.

That is Tim Larkin's entire point in *When Violence Is the Answer*, and it's why we talk so much about deadly force in the previous chapter. Most of the time, you should do everything in your power to flee from danger. Like Jocko said, your first line of defense is your feet and running away. But in those instances where you can't run away, then you must be prepared to stand your ground and use deadly force. In this instance, with your EDC pistol.

One of the things I've learned over my years of teaching

preparedness is that the people who default to smaller options—because they're more concerned about concealment than about capacity or capability—are the same people who are rarely prepared to use deadly force when necessary. They don't train with their firearms. They don't clean them regularly. In more cases than I care to remember, people with this kind of mentality tend to not even keep their pistols loaded. I have seen this with EDC concealed-carry firearms *and* pistols maintained for home defense. The gun is in one location; ammunition is in another location. From a self-defense preparedness perspective, this is insanity!

That being said, bigger is not always better. A pistol that is too big for you becomes unwieldy. It increases the risk of malfunction or user error. It brings potentially fatal consequences into play for bystanders and unintended targets because controlling recoil and muzzle flip is more difficult. Technically, you have greater self-defense capacity with a bigger pistol, but your capability has decreased at the same time, depending on your size.

What is best is what fits comfortably in your hand, on your person, or in your bag. I have large hands, so a smaller pistol reduces my self-defense capability because it becomes harder for me to manipulate. My hands swallow it up. My trigger finger doesn't sit naturally where it should on the trigger. My gun hand manipulating the slide and the magazine release, my support hand managing muzzle flip and recoil—they're all out of whack. It's the firearms version of swinging a Wiffle bat as an adult—your hands overwhelm the size of the bat because it's not optimized for your size, thus you increase your chances of missing the ball. Needless to say, this is suboptimal for self-defense.

My preferred EDC pistol is a Sig Sauer P365-XMacro with 17+1 round capability, mounted with a Red Dot optic.* It's a compact pistol that is compensated to reduce muzzle flip and is only one inch thick, which increases comfort and concealability. But this hasn't compromised its capacity of 9mm rounds, which is usually what happens when a manufacturer makes one of their pistols smaller. It's worth noting that I have carried different models of Sig Sauer pistols over the years, of various sizes. Before this, I carried the P320 XCarry, which is the middle of the three basic sizes in the P320 line. I've also carried the larger, so-called full-size P320 X5 in the past, and liked it, especially the twenty-one-round extended clip option. But *for me*, as of this writing, the shorter length and lighter weight of the P365-XMacro is what I'm looking for. I don't overwhelm it with my larger-than-average hand size, it works with the configuration of my EDC bag (which I'll talk about later), it fits with how I walk through the world, and it doesn't print to the outside world against my clothes when I wear it under my shirt in the appendix carry position.

Always ensure you test and evaluate different pistol and

---

*17+1 means that the magazine holds seventeen rounds, with one in the chamber.

holster configurations for different environments. Too often, people approach EDC as if there is one end-all, be-all solution. The reality is we work different schedules, with different routines, and most certainly in different environments. So what you wear, how you wear it—whether you're in a suit versus board shorts—are always considerations you need to take into account. Just as I used specific equipment for specific missions, so should you when lining out your EDC pistol setup.

Remember that accessories are mostly interchangeable and adaptable across platforms. I see many people using Red Dot optics on guns that don't have lights attached. Do you work nights or go out mostly in the evening? Then you might want to look at your most likely and most dangerous courses of action and what pistol is going to be the best solution for those scenarios. For me, a handheld light option in my bag or fanny pack is a perfect way to strike the balance between utility and quickly distinguishing friend from foe in a self-defense situation.

KNIVES

There are two basic categories of knives for everyday carry: tactical knives and survival knives. Tactical knives are meant primarily for fighting. Survival knives are meant primarily for things like chopping and sawing and skinning. The two have a lot in common when it comes to grip construction and blade shape variety, but where they differ most is in blade composition.

The best tactical knives typically have fixed blades (that means they don't fold) made of stainless steel that is coated to make them less visible and more corrosion resistant. They also tend to have longer, finer points and slightly thinner, straighter blades that hold their edge better. This makes them better for stabbing, slicing, and cutting—essential characteristics of a knife being used in self-defense.

Survival knives also tend to have a bias toward fixed blades. The best ones are always full tang, which means the metal blade runs the entire length of the handle; it's not just mounted into the top half of the handle. This makes the whole knife incredibly sturdy, which is essential in a survival situation. The blade on a survival knife is also usually thicker and more durable than those on a tactical knife because the expectation is that they're going to take a lot of punishment out there in the elements chopping, sawing, hacking, and skinning—essential survival activities like that.

That being said, in recent decades the knife industry has moved toward hybrid models to serve the EDC needs of the survival and preparedness community. Shorter folding knives featuring sturdy multifunction blades and clip mounts that make them easy to wear inside a pants pocket are by far the most popular styles being offered. The design focus of these knives has been low profile, low visibility, easy portability, a quick and easy opening mechanism, and blade construction that suits everyday use but includes a point and an edge that are serviceable in a self-defense scenario.

Carrying in Foreign Countries

It's illegal in many countries, even semi-permissive countries, to travel into them carrying certain kinds of knives. If your personal safety and self-defense concerns are pressing enough, the way around that, according to Ed Calderon, a longtime expert in counternarcotics and organized crime in Mexico, is to go to a big box store like Walmart and buy a plastic-handle paring knife with a 3.5- to 4-inch blade. Stores sell them right in the kitchen accessories aisle, next to vegetable peelers and garlic presses, for three dollars. And here's the kicker, according to Calderon: many of these cheap paring knives outperform high-end folding knives in key survival tasks. For the price of a fancy coffee, you can have an effective concealed-carry fixed-blade knife anywhere in the world.

With that understanding, you need to decide for yourself whether your preparedness needs require a dedicated tactical knife for self-defense and a dedicated survival knife for everything else, or if you can comfortably and confidently get by with a hybrid-style knife that was designed with EDC considerations in mind.[*]

---

[*]We went through that process at Fieldcraft Survival and partnered with Montana Knife Company (MKC) to leverage our collective expertise and

Jack Carr, the bestselling author and former Navy SEAL, carries both. He has a folding knife from Half Face Blades that he uses exclusively for cutting rope, opening boxes, clearing small branches, and other similar tasks that he does all the time while living in Utah. He also has an Amtac Northman fixed blade that he carries exclusively for self-defense. By carrying both and assigning them dedicated uses, he ensures that his fighting blade never gets dull.

Like with pistols, the key to selecting the right EDC knife (or knives) for you is comfort. The grip has to feel good in your hand. The knife as a whole can't be too heavy or too light. The blade has to be long enough for you to apply appropriate leverage for essential tasks. And if you choose a folding knife, the opening and folding mechanisms need to match your grip strength, so that if you have weak hands or arthritic fingers, for example, then the knife isn't so difficult to open that it becomes a liability in high-stress self-defense situations.

When I was on active duty, I carried a full-time Winkler or Strider MT blade that was fixed and on my plate carrier. But I also had a folder in my pocket for everyday utility like cutting zip ties and paracord, even opening Meals Ready to Eat (MREs). Remember, with comfort and capacity comes confidence, and with confidence comes capability. You want as much

---

design the Fieldcraft Survival EDC blade, which can do both self-defense and survival very well. In addition, at the time of publication, we have also designed several different knives that are both hybrid and survival knives.

of all those as you can reasonably get when it comes to self-defense.

Nonlethal Options

Every law enforcement agency in the country has what is called a force continuum. It establishes and codifies how and when the escalation of force should occur when a law enforcement officer deals with a criminal suspect. It can go from zero to gun instantly if a suspect is waving a gun around or holding a knife to someone's throat. But if someone is just drunk and belligerent and making vague threats with slurred speech, that person should be confronted and neutralized using some lesser degree of force.

To assist officers in that regard, law enforcement agencies issue them a host of nonlethal weapons, including various kinds of batons, tasers, pepper sprays, and flashlights. In the civilian world, we have the same kind of optionality and an even greater incentive to use it.

STUN GUNS AND SPRAYS

For reasons that aren't totally clear, and are frankly irrelevant, outside of law enforcement, tools like stun guns and pepper spray have typically been a woman's go-to weapon of choice. And while millions of women have used both these self-defense tools effectively and successfully for as long as they have existed, there is no reason to believe that they aren't equally useful for men.

Stun guns and sprays are obviously different to the extent that one uses electricity and the other uses a chemical irritant to do their job, but we talk about them together because of what that job is: to repel. Stun guns and sprays are fundamentally self-defense repellants. They do that by creating distance, in the case of stun guns, and keeping distance, in the case of sprays.

Stun guns *create* distance because, for the gun to work, it has to make physical contact with the threat, which means, by definition, that there is little to no space between you.* The best place to target on the body of an attacker is the torso—from the neck to the hips—ideally where there are lots of nerve endings and large muscle groups. This includes the shoulder, the hip, the stomach, and the groin. These areas, when targeted, will give you maximum effect in terms of stopping power. Once you've deployed your stun gun and stopped your attacker, those next moments give you the chance to create space, flee to safety, or establish an advantageous position and escalate the use of force to fully neutralize the threat. But make no mistake, you will only have moments. Average recovery time from a normal stun gun attack is a few seconds. That is the limitation of stun guns. They're very effective, but the effect is short-lived.

*The exception is the TASER gun, which shoots out electrodes that attach to an attacker's clothing. Still, the range on a TASER is fifteen feet at the farthest.

Sprays, on the other hand, have a significantly longer effect—anywhere from fifteen to forty-five minutes—no matter which kind of spray you're talking about. When we talk about sprays for self-defense, the names you'll hear most often are mace, pepper spray, and bear spray. They used to be quite different chemically, but they have evolved and converged over time to all just be different names for pepper spray, which itself is a kind of tear gas designed for personal use.

The primary active ingredient in all sprays today is capsaicin, derived from a group of plants that includes chilies, which severely irritates the eyes of humans and overwhelms the olfactory senses of bears and other scent-dominant predators. The purpose of sprays is to *keep distance* between you and a looming threat; that's why they have a spray range of anywhere from ten to thirty-five feet. The goal is to repel the threat by stopping it before it can reach you, and then, like with stun guns, for you to use that time to flee or get the upper hand.

What distinguishes one spray from another, specifically what separates pepper spray from bear spray (Mace is now just a brand that offers both), is the concentration of capsaicin in the spray and its dispersal pattern out of the can. This, in turn, should help you decide if and when you should carry one of them.

Pepper spray comes in small canisters (most states have laws about the maximum size and potency of pepper spray for personal use) that are designed for easy concealment and portability. They spray concentrated narrow jets of a capsaicin solution, usually with a range of ten to eighteen feet, and are meant to target the eyes of the attacker.

Bear spray is typically two to three times stronger than pepper spray, and canisters have a range of up to thirty-five feet, which is double the reach of many pepper spray brands. This seems like an obvious advantage for self-defense, until you understand that bear spray disperses like a fire extinguisher, sending a large cloud of spray out in front of you in the direction (presumably) of the bear or other predator. The reason for this is that bears have very large heads, and the goal with bear spray is to get coverage of the entire face to increase the chances that the spray gets inhaled.

There are a few problems with this when it comes to repelling a human threat, however. One, a cloud of spray is easier for a human attacker to circumvent; two, if the wind is wrong, the cloud could come back on you, putting you in an even worse position; and three, a cloud of spray is by definition less concentrated than a jet of spray, so even if the human threat does get some in their eyes, the chances of them clearing it fairly quickly and not being debilitated is significantly higher. In addition, bear spray comes in canisters that are often three to four times larger than pepper spray cans, which makes them much less portable and concealable, and therefore much less efficient for EDC self-defense.

When deciding whether to add a stun gun or a spray to your EDC loadout, your environment is really going to be the main consideration. If you're going to a frat party, a stun gun makes a lot of sense. Pepper spray would affect too many bystanders, and understanding that the place is going to be crowded, shoulder to shoulder, you'll likely have the proximity necessary for a stun gun to be an effective nonlethal self-defense tool. On the other hand, if you're a runner who does eight miles every morning at dawn, or you're going camping up in the Pacific Northwest, maybe a canister of pepper spray or bear spray is what you should have with you. Regardless, the thing to remember about stun guns and sprays is that their job is not to injure or kill, but to repel by creating or keeping distance, which gives you the time you need to get away.

ALARMS

There are situations in self-defense where escape is not the only consideration; in some scenarios you also need detection. Situations where maybe you can't get to your knife or your stun gun, situations where it's too crowded or windy to use pepper spray, or situations where an attacker is trying to rob you or relocate you from a place without being detected. In scenarios like that, your greatest weapon is often not lethal, but instead something very loud—some kind of loud, piercing, attention-getting alarm.

It can be as simple as an old-fashioned whistle you wear around your neck or as high tech as a personal safety alarm that clips to your pocket or your keychain and emits a loud, high-pitched sound when pressed, which can be heard for blocks or across large parks. (These alarms are also perfect for your children's EDC, whether in their backpack or on their person.) In either case, besides attracting attention and drawing witnesses, alarms such as these have the added benefit of potentially startling your attacker, which could then give you the time and space you need to either run or defend yourself with your EDC pistol, knife, or pepper spray.

It's important to understand as we move into the survival aspect of everyday carry that I'm not suggesting you carry one of each of these things on you wherever you go. However, each of these things should be in your arsenal to swap in and out depending on the circumstance, the environment, and your own instincts about the relative safety of the situation for you and your family. You don't bring a knife to a gunfight, but you also don't bring a gun to a pillow fight.

Knowing when to carry is just as important as knowing what to carry.

Survival

When I train survival in the context of everyday carry, the framework for that training is seventy-two hours. I want you to have, and train with, the things you will need to survive on your own for up to three days exposed to the elements—in the broadest sense of that term—with nothing but what is on your person.

The way to think about this is in short-term scenarios. Being stranded on the side of the road in a remote area late at night in the middle of March with no cell phone signal, having just been injured in a car accident. Getting separated from your group while traveling in a semipermissive foreign country or hiking in the backcountry and finding yourself lost. Being flooded out by a hurricane and getting stuck in a Hurricane Katrina–type situation where the rule of law breaks down.

In these situations, there is a set of things you need to have on you if you want to ensure your survival and make the experience as painless as possible. I'll go through them in the order that can kill you quickest if you don't have them.

Medical

In the lexicon of survival and EDC, medical considerations often go unmentioned, but they are in my opinion a foundational staple of preparedness that should never be overlooked or underresourced. If you or someone in your party is meaningfully injured in a crisis situation, it's going to be up to you to stop the bleeding and treat the wound so that you don't get slowed down more than necessary or, in the worst-case scenario, so that you or someone you love doesn't die.

For that to be possible you have to carry a tourniquet and some kind of individual first aid kit (IFAK) or bleeding control kit that includes a combination of trauma or compression bandages, combat gauze for wound packing, compressed gauze for wound dressing, and medical tape to secure everything.

This medical equipment, which can fit easily into the front pocket of a backpack or in a medium-size purse, gives you the capacity and capability to stop arterial bleeds, treat different kinds of wounds—from lacerations to puncture or cavitation wounds—and address minor burns, scrapes, and cuts that could get infected if they were to go unattended for two or three days.

If you had to pick one item from that list, if you could only afford to buy one, or if you only had room to carry one on your person, hands down it should be a tourniquet. Deep cuts and puncture wounds are scary, but neither is as deadly as an arterial bleed. Like I talked about earlier, you may have just minutes with an arterial bleed before you're done.

That said, I strongly urge you to set yourself up so that your EDC includes the fullest complement of medical equipment possible. In a catastrophe, you have time to find shelter and water and warmth. You don't have that time when you've been gravely wounded.*

Shelter and Fire

All things being equal, and injuries aside, the elements are always the first thing that will get you. You can die from cold exposure, or hypothermia, in less than an hour if enough of your skin is exposed and your core body temperature drops below 80 degrees Fahrenheit. Conversely, you can die from heat exposure, or *hyper*thermia, when your core body temperature

---

*At Fieldcraft Survival, we make small bleeding control kits (BCKs) that have everything you need to stop the bleed, and are neat and tidy and fit conveniently in your EDC.

gets above 103 degrees, in three to four hours and sometimes in as little as ninety minutes.

To insulate yourself from these environmental threats, you should always carry with you a means to create rudimentary shelter and to keep warm. This sounds potentially very complicated, but it's actually very simple from an EDC perspective.

For shelter and a source of warmth, there is really only one option: a Mylar thermal blanket. (You may know it by other names, like a space blanket or emergency blanket.) A Mylar blanket is that thin, shiny, tarp-like material that you will see marathoners wrapped in at the finish line, or accident and fire victims wrapped in on the side of the road. Mylar blankets are amazing in their dual-purpose ability to reflect 90 percent of radiant heat to keep you cool and to retain 90 percent of your body heat to keep you warm. This means they can protect and sustain your core body temperature, functioning as a kind of makeshift shelter from the elements whether you're stranded in the snow in the middle of the night or stuck in the sand in the desert at high noon.

Mylar blankets are also incredibly practical. Open, they typically fold out to a 7.5 ft. by 4 ft. rectangle. But in the package, they're 5 in. by 6 in. by ½ in. and weigh less than a pound, which makes them ultraportable. On top of that, you can buy them in packs for between ten and twenty dollars. If you're serious about preparedness and your EDC, there's really no excuse not to have at least one Mylar blanket on hand for each member of your family, and one in your bag at all times.

Fire solutions in everyday carry are equally straightforward. It's lighters, hurricane matches, and magnesium fire starters. Any one of these three options is perfectly sufficient for creating fire and offering sustained warmth. They are also all lightweight, small, and inexpensive, which makes them perfect for everyday carry.

What separates them is their effectiveness in a given environment. If you live in a windy area or a rainy area, if you live at elevation or in a hurricane zone or in Tornado Alley and it's peak season, that should impact your decision-making. Your environment should be able to tell you whether a basic lighter is enough or if you should include something a little sturdier and more resilient, like hurricane matches. Personally, I typically carry a Bic lighter, which costs a dollar, and when I'm out in the country or going for a hike in the woods with my family, I'll add the fire starter to my bag as a contingency, since starting a fire in the wilderness is usually more complicated than simply putting a Bic lighter to a bunch of logs.

Food and Water

In a seventy-two-hour scenario, food is usually not much of a concern for immediate survival, but if you're diabetic or you have young children with you or you have to keep moving on foot to survive, then it's key to have something in your bag that has decent calories, a sufficient level of sodium, and good available carbs to recruit for quick energy. A couple good-quality protein bars and a few of those small 100- to 200-calorie energy gel packets that cyclists and long-distance runners use is easily enough to sustain you until you can find a more consistent food source.

Water is by far the most pressing concern. Three days without water is just about the limit for the average human body, and that time shrinks with exertion and exposure. There is individual size "survival water" in packets and cans that you can buy and that don't take up too much space in an EDC bag, but water is disproportionately heavier by volume than most other things its size; and once you've drunk it, it's gone. The more efficient move is to include a solution for storing and purifying water.

The best option that combines those functions is something like the GRAYL GeoPress water purifier bottle that pushes a filter through untreated water and both cleans it and kills off dangerous pathogens, all in one container. The GRAYL system isn't cheap, however. So, if cost is an issue, the next best option is to split those storage and purification functions and try to find value. For water storage, look either for a collapsible food-grade silicone water bottle that holds a rigid structure when extended and filled, or a thin plastic, capped bladder that rolls up when empty. Collapsible bottles tend to have slightly greater capacity on average and they're easier to drink from, but the bladders (even larger varieties) take up significantly less space in a bag when they're empty and stored. When you're deciding between storage options, this is the calculus you will have to make.

This leads us to purification. There are a number of filtration and purification systems on the market, but the simplest and most portable for personal use are chlorine dioxide tablets. You can buy them by the pack for less than twenty dollars. They fit easily in the interior pockets of any bag. One tablet purifies a liter of drinking water, and it's effective against viruses, bacteria, and common waterborne parasites like *Giardia* and *Cryptosporidium*, which can induce diarrhea and vomiting and accelerate dehydration.

A water purification method is a critical component of EDC for survival—because it doesn't matter which water storage option you choose, or how much water you can collect, if you can't drink any of it.

Illumination

Light will not save your life in a catastrophe, but it can definitely show you the way to safety. Depending on where I am or what I'm doing, I carry either a flashlight or a headlamp, and sometimes both.

Flashlights are the ideal illumination tool when you are scanning your surroundings for threats and obstacles, when you're searching for something, or when you're leading other people through darkness. A flashlight can also double as a weapon and a signaling device, which makes carrying one that much more valuable. There is a variety of powerful, sturdy compact flashlights on the market now, so finding one that fits your budget, your hand, and your available space has never been easier.

A headlamp is a mission-essential piece of equipment. It's an ideal solution when you want to have both hands free and you don't need whatever benefit might be gained from having your head movement offset from the movement of the light source. A headlamp is hugely advantageous for looking under the hood of your broken-down vehicle at night and being able to see into tight spots as you maneuver with tools. It's helpful when you're cutting through brush and footing is bad. And it's ideal when you've drawn your pistol and have it presented scanning for threats.* In fact, it has the added benefit of replacing night sights and lights on the pistol itself, which allows you to maintain an EDC pistol that is lighter and lower profile.

In the most robust version of your EDC, I would argue that having a headlamp as your primary light source and a flashlight as your contingency is the way to go. I'm a fan of both Petzl headlamps and SureFire tactical lights, but having either is good. And whichever you choose, just remember to check and replace its batteries regularly and carry an extra set with you, just in case.

Signaling

If you're lost or stuck somewhere, everything we've talked about so far will almost certainly keep you alive for seventy-two hours, but if you want to be found or *un*stuck, you'll need to be able to signal rescue personnel on the ground and in the

---

*Most gunfights in self-defense scenarios occur at night.

air to alert them to your position. Fortunately, you already have things in your EDC bag that can do that. At night, a fire is visible from the air. At night and in low light, the beam of a flashlight can be seen from quite a distance. In daylight, the reflective side of a Mylar emergency blanket can catch the sun's rays and be seen from the air and the ground. And at any time of day or night, a loud whistle can be heard for miles.

There is a dedicated tool for signaling, however, that is both small enough and ridiculously effective enough to warrant being included in your EDC bag. It's called a signal mirror. In the military, we used signal mirrors made with glass that, on a clear day with the sun well above the horizon, could be seen from a hundred miles away. The only downside to the glass version of a signal mirror is its vulnerability to cracking or shattering. That's why the best option for maximizing survival capability is a signal mirror made out of durable stainless steel. They don't have quite the range of the glass mirrors, but they can still be seen for many miles.

Signaling mirrors are sold with survival kits in mind, so they are inexpensive, they come in compact sizes (typically 2 in. by 3 in. and 3 in. by 5 in.), and they include accessories like a lanyard that allows you to hang the mirror around your neck or tie it to your bag. It sounds a little far-fetched, but it's a very real possibility that, of all the stuff that makes up your EDC, a six-dollar credit card–shaped piece of stainless steel could be the thing that saves your life.

My Everyday Carry

This is an inventory of my EDC. Depending on what I'm doing or where I'm going or who I'm with, I may carry all this or a scaled-down version. In all cases, self-defense and medical considerations are paramount.

Sling bag

Fanny pack

Bic lighter

Magnesium fire starter

Sig Sauer P365-XMacro with extra magazine

IFAK

Bleeding control kit (BCK)

- Hemostat gauze

- 4-in. compression bandage

- Nitrile gloves

- Medical tape

Sharpie

Ballpoint pen and small pad

Hand sanitizer

Montana fixed blade in a Kydex holster with a belt clip

Benchmade or Viking Tactics folding knife (in the bag)

Bexar Goods Co. leather wallet

SOF-T tourniquet in a tourniquet holder

SureFire V1 Vampire flashlight with white light and infrared illumination capability

Petzl headlamp

THE LESSER KNOWN ELEMENTS OF EVERYDAY CARRY

EDC considerations are dominated by the things you choose to carry every day for the purpose of self-defense and survival, but EDC is not fully defined by those things. It extends beyond *what* you carry, to what you carry it in, what you wear, and how you carry yourself. Those factors are all part of EDC and key variables in the preparedness equation.

Bags

Like pistols and knives, your EDC bags have to be comfortable. They can't be burdensome or cumbersome. They can't be too heavy or too flimsy. You have to like the feeling of wearing them and you have to be comfortable enough getting in and out of them that retrieving items under stress becomes nothing more than a matter of muscle memory.

There is no wrong *kind* of bag. There is only the wrong bag for what you are carrying. If you like the security and even weight distribution of a backpack, carry a backpack. If you prefer the streamlined look of a European man satchel, by all means. The only thing that matters is that the bag has enough space and compartments for you to easily and reliably access the tools of self-defense and survival without having to stop and dig around to find them, wasting valuable seconds in high-stress situations.

My main EDC bag is actually a fly-fishing bag. It has a wide single strap with a small, almost fanny-pack-style compartment in the middle that allows me to wear the bag comfortably across my back and still have quick access to a couple essential items. And because of that single strap, I can easily sling the bag around to my front when I need other, bigger items, where the bag presents almost like a chest rig.

That is the bag I carry for the more robust version of my EDC. If I'm scaling down because I'm going to the beach or to a party or someplace where the full kit wouldn't make sense, I'll wear a fanny pack that has room for my Sig P365 and/or a folding knife, my tourniquet, and my bleeding control kit. For me, that is the bare minimum for self-defense and survival. And who doesn't love a good fanny pack?

Clothes

If you ever see a picture of a group of Special Operations veterans together in a public setting, you will quickly notice that we are all dressed very similarly. It's like a college fraternity photo—which in some ways makes sense, since we are a fraternity, one with a common set of values and a common understanding of the power and importance of preparedness.

We all wear hats and sunglasses. Hats provide protection from the sun. In colder climates, they trap body heat, half of which gets lost through the top of our head. Sunglasses give us an extra layer of protection from the sun's rays and allow us to see better in bright daylight. They also hide where we're looking, so bad actors can never be certain if they're being watched and tracked. The other reason I wear sunglasses—Oakley M Frames in particular—is the ballistic protection they offer against shrapnel and flying debris. In the military, they saved my eyes on multiple occasions.

We all tend to wear multiple layers, including an untucked, short-sleeved, button-up collared shirt and some kind of jacket. The short sleeves give an attacker less to grab on to. The untucked shirt allows for carrying a pistol in any number of configurations without it printing too obviously to an outside observer, and it provides for easier access when we have to pull it. The jacket offers another layer of warmth, another layer of concealment, and an additional set of pockets to store things.

We all tend to wear belts and sturdy pants or shorts with

multiple pockets. This creates a sturdy base to support a holstered pistol, a sheathed fixed-blade knife, and a clipped-on tourniquet without having to worry about our pants falling down. In addition, a belt can be used as an improvised tourniquet, so if we find ourselves in a mass casualty situation, we can help more than one person.

We all tend to wear sturdy shoes or boots with reinforced, rugged soles with plenty of grip. This allows us to run, to climb, or to scramble at a moment's notice without having to worry about trading our flip-flops or slip-ons for shoes with actual support. I love Salomon shoes for every day wear and Crispi hiking boots for more rugged terrain.

These choices are not fashion statements. They are preparedness choices. They are items of clothing that allow us to more effectively carry items for self-defense and survival, which can save lives—ours, our loved ones, and innocent members of our community. Like I learned overseas, if your survival is entirely in your own hands and you haven't dressed the part, then you will be on the back foot from the jump and you may never get off it.

Attitude

If there's one thing I've learned over twenty years in military and intelligence service in war zones and hostile territory, it's that how you carry yourself is truly your first line of defense. When you stand tall, when you stay alert, when you are aware of everything around you, when you look like you know what you're doing and how to handle yourself, violent threats tend to find you less often.

Not only that, but when you carry yourself that way, you will begin to *feel that way*, and then you will start to act that way. It's just the way the mind works. If you want to be less sad, smile more. The smile comes *before* the happiness. There's an old saying, "Fake it 'til you make it." It's true. Project confidence and competence, display capacity and capability—even if you're not totally there yet—and soon enough, you will feel and be all those things. And being all those things will make projecting them effortless and unconscious. It becomes a flywheel, of sorts, that spins off many positive things including, most importantly, preparedness.

6

MOBILITY

On the night of August 29, 2021, the sixteenth anniversary of Hurricane Katrina, a Category 4 hurricane with 150-mile-per-hour sustained winds (30 mph stronger than Katrina) made landfall on the coast of Louisiana. Named Ida by the World Meteorological Organization, the storm had only been classified as a hurricane two days before it made landfall, and it wasn't until the day before that it intensified from a Category 1 to a Category 4, which it did in the space of about six hours.

The fast-developing nature of the storm put Louisiana officials at a disadvantage. But having learned their lesson from Katrina, they scrambled to act as quickly as possible to avoid previous mistakes. Governor John Bel Edwards declared a state of emergency the day the storm hit Cuba and officially became a hurricane. The mayor of New Orleans, LaToya Cantrell, issued a mandatory evacuation order for residents outside the levee protection system on the morning of August 28 when the storm began to rapidly intensify and to track more directly toward the city.*

Within hours, store shelves emptied of bread, water, batteries, and canned goods—staples of survival. Lines at the gas pump stretched for blocks, emptying out filling stations across the state. Traffic was gridlocked for miles on the three main arteries headed west, east, and north out of southern Louisiana. By the morning of August 30, hundreds of thousands of residents along the Gulf Coast would be displaced, many for months, some permanently.

Where did they all go? It's a good question—one that many residents didn't have an answer to before they got in their cars, filled up their tanks, picked up some groceries, and hit the road. It was a question they answered on the fly, with desperate phone calls to relatives and friends who lived out of state, or to motels that might have vacancies or discount rates for people fleeing a natural disaster. It was situational triage at its most frantic—because most people, despite living in a flood zone and a hurricane hotspot, were not prepared for something sudden and catastrophic like a mandatory evacuation from a hurricane.

*Ida had intensified so quickly there was no time to issue an orderly mandatory evacuation order that included residents inside the levee protection system. To do so would have produced total chaos.

I've talked often about having the ability to assess and avoid danger. To flee from threats. To escape catastrophe. To bug out, as we call it. But I haven't talked a lot about *how* you literally do that and with what kind of equipment in mind. In a worst-case scenario, one of the surest tactics to avoid becoming a casualty is having a well-rehearsed plan of escape and evasion, and a well-equipped vehicle. In other words, loading up your car, truck, or motorcycle to get off the X (in this case, the crisis site) and increase the probability of your survival.

THE START POINT FOR MOBILITY

In preparedness, mobility is all about extending your capacity. The extension of your capacity increases the quantity of essential items you can carry, thus potentially increasing your overall capability, not just for putting time and distance between yourself and danger, but ultimately for survival. In this way, mobility is as much a tool of preparedness as it is a principle, as Clay Croft, the founder of the overland adventure video series Expedition Overland, has taught me. "Mobility is a means of increasing and maintaining your freedom to move," Clay teaches. The freedom to move is an essential aspect of preparedness because eventually, no matter how robust or secure your homestead is, no matter what kind of survival situation you find yourself in, you're going to have to move. Whether it's to get supplies, flee an encroaching threat, rescue a member of your family, or a hundred other scenarios, as Clay has explained to people in his videos, survival doesn't mean staying put forever, it means staying alive and thriving for as long as possible.

The only real limit on your ability to extend and escape, on your freedom to move is the size of your mobility platform. Too small, like a compact car, and you'll struggle with capacity, with your ability to navigate varied and rugged terrain, and thus with your capability to self-sustain for an extended period of time. Too big, like a cargo van or a semitruck, and you'll be able to carry enough to take care of a village, but you will struggle with capability because you'll be slow and tethered to paved roads with wide lanes. This will make moving on single-track and back roads to get off grid nearly impossible.*

For most people, the sweet spot for mobility is somewhere in the middle, and the spectrum of options is thankfully very large—from all-wheel drive sedans to fully built rigs. Regardless of where you land on that spectrum, however, there are two areas that you need to have squared away to consider yourself meaningfully prepared: survival and first aid.

---

*For those who are single or who have small families and are adept on two wheels, at the end of this chapter I've included an extended section on building out a motorcycle as a bug-out rig.

SURVIVAL

Survival breaks down very simply: shelter, warmth, water, food, communications. Most of that should sound familiar. We talked about these very things in the previous chapter. Here's the difference: now we're talking about more than just you in the immediate term. We're talking about the extension of those capabilities over the long haul for yourself and for your family. We're talking about what's necessary, not just so that they survive, but so that they can function effectively for extended periods of time. The key here is being able to displace from a bad situation to a good one, and thriving along the way.

Shelter

Here's a simple mnemonic to help you remember what you need for shelter on the road, for short or extended periods of time: IOU. In. On. Under. You need something to shelter and sleep IN, something to sleep ON, and something to sleep UNDER. This isn't just a comfort consideration, but a survival consideration, as exposure to the elements in extreme environments, both hot and cold, can easily kill you.

In

The reality is that your vehicle is a shelter on wheels. With fuel, it's essentially a climate-controlled home that will keep you comfortable, but also offer regulated temperature in the most extreme conditions. Have a shelter and sleeping setup in mind for recreation and the worst-case scenario for you and your family. If you have a smaller vehicle, think about using alternative means of extending your shelter. This could be awnings, putting the front seats down, or modifying your vehicle with rear-seat delete. Goose Gear based in California makes a great setup that turns the space in your vehicle into usable sleeping and utility storage space.

On

Rooftop camping is becoming more popular for overland enthusiasts nationwide. Companies like Eezi-Awn, Alu-Cab, and iKamper all offer reliable solutions using the empty rooftop of your truck, SUV, and even a standard car to provide an easy pop-up tent shelter. For a family this is the perfect balance of not overloading your mobility platform's load capacity, but offering IN and ON solutions to spread the family out. The drawback is most aren't climate-controlled, and they are limited on sleep capacity and space.

When it comes to the individual sleep configuration, there is an endless variety of sleeping pads on the market, from the inflatable to the insulated and the memory foam–filled ones, too. The prices run the gamut, so you can decide how important comfort is and how much you're willing to spend to achieve it. The key is understanding how much space they will take up in whatever vehicle you're bugging out in. Some sleeping pads roll up incredibly tight, some are a little bulkier, and some you're better off just laying flat and packing everything else on top of. That's why you can't just order things like this online and expect to be good to go, sight unseen. You'll want to see them and touch them and manipulate them yourself, then make a determination from there. All it is going to cost you is time. And now is when you actually have time to spare.

Under

In a perfect world, you'd have low-profile, down-filled mummy design sleeping bags rated to subfreezing temperatures for everyone in your family. If that's not financially feasible, or you intend for everyone to sleep in the vehicle with an ambient heat source, an alternative covering option could be wool blankets or down comforters. In either case, you should also have at least one Mylar blanket for everyone. Not only are they an ideal contingency for shelter and maintaining body heat, but they also have signaling, water-capture, and first aid functionality. They are an absolute must-have. And when you factor in their low cost, negligible weight, and small footprint, there's really no excuse for not having them in your vehicle at all times.

In Afghanistan, we couldn't be buttoned up in a tent or sleeping bag like that because we needed to be able to react and respond quickly, but we still needed temporary shelter to keep us out of the rain, so we slept under Mad Max chopped Land Rovers for weeks at a time. If you have a taller vehicle with more ground clearance, and you're in a high-threat environment or you're just out of space inside the vehicle itself, then you have a rooftop and shelter right there under your truck. Although not the most comfortable, it will keep you out of the elements; and with the proper side walls like tarps and makeshift attachments, it's just as comfortable as sleeping in a tent.

Warmth

One of the necessities in survival is maintaining a stable core body temperature. Creating a fire is the principal way of keeping your environment warm, with the added benefit of being able to signal both day and night. The minimum start point for warmth, and an item to be sure you have in your mobility platform, is a butane lighter, waterproof hurricane matches, and a magnesium fire starter. Each of these items is small enough and inexpensive enough that you should have multiples of each in your vehicle. In something as compact as a fishing tackle box or a toolbox, you could easily and neatly fit each kind of fire source as well as complementary materials, including tinder and even a small fire-starting log to reduce the time it takes to get a fire going. This way, you don't just have every contingency covered; you have ample redundancy as well.

In addition to fire, what you wear matters in and out of your vehicle. A good outerwear layer is essential for keeping that heat in and maintaining a positive core temperature. A waterproof Gore-Tex layer with a hood is a good idea in this context.

So is a lightweight down puffy jacket. Unlike fire-starting equipment, these apparel items are not cheap,* but they are an important consideration for every member of your travel party because their insulation and warmth allow you to be mobile on foot, away from your mobility platform, for several hours at a time.

Water

There is a "rule of threes" in survival: three hours without shelter, three days without water, three weeks without food. Any one of these can kill you if the conditions are right—or wrong. With the storage capacity available in even a modestly sized vehicle, you should have no less than one to two gallons of clean drinking water per family member onboard at any given time, with the expectation that you'll need to replenish those stores daily for the purposes of drinking, cooking, and hygiene. This means you'll want to have some way to procure, sanitize, and store water at a decent scale.

Procurement

Setting aside the ability to buy bottled water or to collect lake or river water, you'll want a way to capture rainwater as well. You

*Check out Eberlestock, Kuhl, and Fieldcraft Survival for clothing and layering options to keep you insulated and warm.

can use a Mylar blanket for that, like I mentioned, but having a dedicated, collapsible capture system in your rig as the primary means of rainwater capture is ideal. You can also fashion one from a tarp, tent poles, bungee cords, and some kind of funnel mechanism from the catch to whatever storage receptacle you have. Bladders and bottles make perfect capturing vessels for storage and sanitizing.

Sanitation

The surest way to sanitize larger batches of water from natural or unknown sources is to boil it and kill all the waterborne bacteria, viruses, and protozoa. To do that, you bring the water up to a rapid, rolling boil for at least a minute (two to three minutes at higher elevation), and then let it cool naturally before storing. Of course, this means having some kind of pot in your vehicle that can hold a decent amount of water and stand up to an open fire, but you should have some kind of cooking vessel anyway, so this shouldn't be a problem. I'm a big fan of Jetboil setups that use a butane and propane mix, which gets water boiling without a stoked fire.

On the off chance that boiling water isn't an option, be prepared as a contingency to include a bottle of plain, unscented chlorine bleach to disinfect your water. Bleach typically comes in a 6 percent and an 8.25 percent sodium hypochlorite solution, and you'll rarely need to use more than a teaspoon at a time, so make sure you carry the right size bottle for the space available and that you use the right amount based on the quantity of water you're disinfecting (see table below).*

According to the Environmental Protection Agency (EPA), you should stir the bleach into the water and let it sit for at least thirty minutes. The water should still have a slight chlorine odor after the treatment process. If it doesn't, you should repeat the treatment and let the water sit for an additional fifteen minutes. If the water *tastes* too chlorinated, don't dilute it, simply transfer it back and forth between two clean containers, which will help dissipate that chlorine taste.

EPA Water Treatment Protocol with Chlorine Bleach

Volume of Water	Amount of 6% Bleach to Add*	Amount of 8.25% Bleach to Add*
1 quart (or liter)	2 drops	2 drops
1 gallon	8 drops	6 drops
2 gallons	16 drops (¼ tsp)	12 drops (⅛ teaspoon)
4 gallons	⅓ teaspoon	¼ teaspoon
8 gallons	⅔ teaspoon	½ teaspoon

*The Grayl system I talked about in Chapter 5 is also ideal for mobility. Grayl makes an awesome capturing bottle that uses a filter to push through the captured water to sanitize into purified drinking water. I've used this a lot, both on and off my mobility platforms, in remote areas where I had access to natural running water.

One important note: disinfection doesn't work as well with colored or cloudy water. If you find yourself in this situation, let your collected water settle, then filter it through a clean paper towel, cloth, or coffee filter before proceeding with the sanitizing protocol.

If neither boiling nor bleach are available to you, the contingency to the contingency, or the E in your water PACE plan, could be iodine (tablets or drops)* or "solar water disinfection," which involves collecting water in a clear glass or plastic container and setting it out in the sun for at least six hours so the sun's UV rays can kill the microbes that tend to live in untreated water. The World Health Organization has advocated for this treatment method in impoverished, remote areas where clean drinking water is scarce, because it is virtually cost-free.† If you're in a place with abundant sunlight, this can be a cost-free option for you as well.

Storage

If your mobility platform is a truck with good bed capacity and your traveling party is four or more, it's not a bad idea to consider mounting a forty- to seventy-gallon auxiliary water tank against the back of the bed near the cab. They typically take up

---

*Five drops of a 2 percent iodine solution, or tincture, can disinfect a liter of water. Ten drops if the water is cloudy.

†For murky or cloudy water, adding a bit of table salt has been known to help bind sediment particles and make them settle to the bottom of the container, giving the sun a better shot at disinfecting the water.

less than three feet of bed depth with intentional low visibility construction so they sit below the top of the bed line.

If you don't have the space or the need for an affixed tank of that size, the next best option are one- or two-gallon Rotopax water containers that are thicker and sturdier than fuel containers, but have the same flat, modular, angular design that make them stackable, reducing wasted space. You can also buy mounting hardware for these packs that secure them to your vehicle frame and allow you to double and triple stack them for maximum capacity.*

Food

Your food stores are where we see the power of extension in its purest form when it comes to mobility. In the previous chapter, I talked about having a couple calorically dense protein bars in your bag to help push through that seventy-two-hour survival window. In your vehicle, you should have at least a couple *boxes*, along with nutrient-dense, easily storable foods like nuts, jerky, and energy gels.

The average adult burns between 1,600 and 3,000 calories per day depending on sex and body type, without doing any strenuous activity at all. In a survival situation, you can imagine that

---

*One of my favorite setups is using a custom aluminum bed from Bowen Customs outside Denver, Colorado. With a storage drawer and cabinet system with storage for days, it integrates into your flatbed for easy access.

number goes up quite a bit, and it doesn't take too many days in a row at a significant calorie deficit for muscle weakness and brain fog to start setting in. Which means it's important to fill your tanks whenever you can and, when that's not possible, to at least manage your calorie deficit so you can be effective in protecting your family and continuing to extend the time and distance between you and whatever dangerous situation you're escaping.

Communications

There's a weird tension in survival and preparedness between being able to escape and wanting to be found. While we have talked for the most part in this chapter about getting away and putting distance between yourself and deadly threats, the ability to be found or to find those who are also fleeing (like Louisiana residents from Hurricane Ida) is equally important. While your cell phone is always going to be your first option, to communicate reliably in a crisis environment requires access to and familiarity with technologies and modalities that don't depend on cellular phone networks and cell tower infrastructure.

The most rudimentary form of communication is signaling. We talked about this last chapter with regard to Mylar blankets and fire, and they remain effective methods in the context of mobility.* The downside is that they are one-way forms of

*Adding green foliage to a fire produces massive plumes of white smoke that can be visible for miles during daylight.

the most basic, most broadly receivable communication. Which is to say, you don't get to choose who you're talking to or what you're saying to them. You are telling anyone within eyeshot, "Here I am." That's it. And if you're lost or injured, or both, that can be enough. But sometimes, you need your communication to be more individually aimed and discreet. Sometimes you only want certain people to know where you are or where you're going.

For these situations, for communicating over the horizon, a satellite-based communications system is a great tool. If you have a clear view of the sky, a portable unit like a Garmin in-Reach allows you to communicate your location, to share way-points on your path, and to SMS chat with anyone who also has an inReach, or who has an SMS-enabled phone number or an email address. Basically, you can reach anyone.

You must remember, preparedness isn't just about survival in the strictest sense. It isn't just about not falling victim to a threat or not dying in a dangerous situation. It's about persisting in the face of catastrophe and being able to thrive in austere environments with your family and within your community. (We'll talk more about community in Chapter 7—The Homestead.) A big part of that is keeping lines of communication open—figuratively and, in this case, literally.

FIRST AID

When I think about that concept of extension in the context of first aid, I think about the difference between what a person can carry and what a vehicle can carry. It's the difference between a paramedic and an ambulance. If you or someone you love were injured, which would you want pulling up to the scene: a paramedic with his bag or a paramedic in an ambulance full of treatment options with the ability to transport you to a higher level of care? I think the answer's pretty obvious, which is why the primary consideration for first aid in mobility goes beyond simply extending the capability for survival in the long term, and focuses heavily on extending the capacity for short-term survival of acute trauma from catastrophic accidents with multiple or mass casualties.

This is, in my opinion, the most important area of vehicular preparedness to pay attention to since, of all potential catastrophic events you might face in your life, a vehicle accident is by far the most likely. In 2019, the last year with normal behavior patterns before COVID-19 changed things, there were 6.74 million reported car accidents in the United States alone. That's more than eighteen thousand per day, nearly thirteen per minute. And 6 percent of these accidents were fatal. The average American drives more than fourteen thousand miles per year. The odds of being involved in a bad accident at some point in your life, or witnessing one, or being first on scene to one . . . they're significant. Your preparation should be as well.

Tourniquets

Imagine, for a moment, that you are a family of four driving down a busy highway on the way to your in-laws for Sunday dinner when another family of four in a van coming from the other direction loses control, crosses the median, and T-bones you between the driver-side door and the left rear quarter panel at sixty-five miles per hour. The impact and your momentum send you into a spin that you try to recover from, but when you hit a guardrail it causes your vehicle to roll twice before landing on the roof. You're alive, you're conscious, but you're disoriented. Still, before your vehicle has even come to a stop and the sound of tearing metal has ceased, before you're able to gather what has happened or where the other vehicle is, there is one fact you already know to be true: there are sixteen extremities in your vehicle to account for. Four sets of arms and legs, each with a major artery that, when lacerated by external objects or a fractured bone, can bleed out in minutes.

Because of that, I recommend you have no fewer than four tourniquets securely staged in your vehicle. Even if you don't have a family, even if it's just you, it's still a good idea to have multiple tourniquets onboard. There's no worse feeling than coming upon a multivehicle, mass-casualty accident and having to choose who you help and, by extension, who you don't.

But that is just the capacity aspect of first aid. The key component to first aid in vehicles is ready access, which defines your *capability* in the moment. Being able to reach out, upside down, whether you're the one traumatized or the one who will be rendering aid, and grab lifesaving equipment is absolutely critical. It's the reason I designed all of our equipment at Fieldcraft Survival to be readily accessible on your visor panel, the back of your seats, or at your feet using our mobility duffels. What good is your lifesaving equipment if it's locked in a trunk that is now inaccessible because your vehicle is upside down?

Vehicle Trauma Response Kit (VTRK)

A good vehicle trauma response kit covers as many people as can comfortably (or regularly) ride in your vehicle. Properly built out, a VTRK includes all the staples of first aid designed to address a broad range of critical needs beyond arterial bleeds (which is the role of the tourniquet). It includes multiple, variable-sized bandages, compressed gauze, hemostatic combat gauze, burn dressings, vented chest seals, aluminum eye shields, variable-sized SAM splints, nasopharyngeal airways, trauma shears, splints, medical tape, at least two pairs of nitrile gloves, and a Sharpie marker to indicate to first responders who has been treated, what for, and what with.

The ultimate size of your VTRK will vary based on the size of your family and the extent to which you personally want to be prepared for what you might face on the roads. What should not change are the types of wounds this kit will allow you to treat if you find yourself in or at the scene of any kind of bad accident: burns, lacerations, cavitational wounds, punctures, breaks, chest wounds, collapsed airways, eye trauma, and of course, all manner of bleeds. These wounds can be fatal, so you need to be prepared to treat them with that same level of urgency.

But even those wounds that aren't fatal, if they're left untreated or poorly treated, could significantly limit the mobility of your traveling party, especially in scenarios that are catastrophic at a societal level. As SEALs learn in BUD/S and Green Berets learn at the Q Course,* your team is only as strong as your weakest member. So, if you're trying to flee violent civil unrest, for example, or a tsunami, or a volcanic eruption or a mushroom cloud and your twelve-year-old son breaks his wrist running to your vehicle and you aren't able to splint it, his agony is going to force you to slow down over difficult terrain. Like I said at the very beginning of this chapter, the virtue of a robust mobility platform is being able to put as much time and distance between you and a threat as possible. The last thing you want is to be slowed down by something completely unrelated to the vehicle itself.

Accessibility

When I was in my early twenties, I was following my good friend John and Special Forces Team Sergeant Walker and his wife as they rode on his motorcycle on a beautiful Saturday

---

*The Q Course is the informal name for the US Army's Special Forces Qualifications Course, a year-long, multiphase training program that determines who gains entry to the Army Special Forces.

morning in Spring Lake, North Carolina. It was a crisp, clear day and there was no inclement weather or weird road obstructions. But then, out of nowhere, a car pulled out of a gas station, and my buddy and his wife T-boned them going over forty miles per hour. She flew from the back of the bike and tragically died instantly. My buddy was gravely injured, but he was still moving. From the driver's seat of my Jeep Wrangler, I reached behind me for my med kit, but it was adhered to the back of my seat with MOLLE attachments. These MOLLE attachments meant it was permanently adhered to the seat by woven nylon and to remove it would take too much time. So I had to reach into the med pouch, pull out all the loose contents, and run to Walker's side with a pile of equipment to render aid.

Not ideal, especially in a high-stress situation where seconds counted. I lost precious time in that moment by not having a readily accessible first aid kit that I could pull and grab. By the time I got to Walker he was already slipping away. A few minutes later, he would die as I held his hand loading him onto a Flight-for-Life helicopter to the closest trauma hospital, where his immediate family would be waiting to receive him. Was the delay reaching for my kit the difference between life and death? Probably not. But the reality is that when first responders are minutes away, seconds count. It's the motivation behind the Mobility Panel and Mobility Pack I designed for my company to allow you to rip away using a Velcro attachment, with a pull cord to readily access lifesaving first aid equipment. To arrive with contents intact, and be able to methodically treat a casualty or yourself is imperative in mobile survival.

Since then, I have made accessibility a fundamental tenet of first aid for the mobility platform. It's not enough just to have the right stuff if you can't get to it quickly enough to use it effectively. That's why I go deep on easy access in my own rig and with the medical gear I design. I have a streamlined bleeding control kit with a tourniquet in a pair of pouches that wrap around the passenger-side visor panel. I have different trauma kits and lesser first aid items in their own pouches that Velcro to a bag that hangs around the passenger seat headrest and can be quickly ripped away without having to unbuckle your seatbelt. The bag itself can be unbuckled, zipped up, and worn like a backpack, making me immediately more capable of rendering first aid in situations where maybe I can't get my truck closer to the person or people in distress.

This is how I do it, and how I train people to set up first aid kits and medical bags inside their respective mobility platforms. You don't have to do it my way. You can, and should, adapt your setup to what your vehicle allows and for how you move. What matters is that you have ready access to your equipment so that your capability matches your capacity to render aid to those in need.

BUGGING OUT, FOR REAL

Survival and first aid are the principal pillars of preparedness in the mobility space, but they are only the beginning when it comes to outfitting a vehicle for bugging out indefinitely at a moment's notice. Unlike fleeing a natural disaster like the displaced victims of Hurricane Ida, often the impulse to bug out is triggered by a sense for some sort of looming man-made catastrophe. Those of us with fully loaded bug-out rigs are able to envision our worlds upended by civil unrest, by a collapse of institutions, of law and order, of fiat currency, and the odds are high enough in our estimation that being fully prepared to bug out doesn't seem all that crazy. If anything, not being prepared even a little bit seems like the most insane thing in the world.

All of which is to say, if you think that you might have to bug out one of these days in the not-too-distant future, and you want to start building up your bug-out rig for that eventuality, then you really need to start doing some thinking and some planning. It's not so simple as buying boxes of MREs and shotgun shells and driving your truck as far out into the middle of nowhere as you can get just to be away from civilization.*

*It's one of the reasons we've decided to teach courses like Bug-Out Planning at Fieldcraft Survival. Sure, it's not as exciting as Gun Fighter or our Mobility Experience, but it's exactly the type of "attention to detail" course you need to comprehensively and methodically plan the worst-case-scenario bug out.

Mike's Bug-Out Rig Loadout

Vehicle—Ford F-350, Bowen Customs nine-foot flatbed, Scout Kenai camper shell, Carli suspension, 37-inch tires.

Food—Cook Partner 2 Burner, iKamper Disco, 50-75L refrigerator, Pelican Air Case 1637 as a pantry (can also store Mountain House Meals with no maintenance), propane tank and mount. Table and chairs.

Water—One to two gallons of water storage per person, per day. Rotopax or auxiliary tank. Note: you need water catch, pump, and filter to refill.

Shelter—I O U (IN ON UNDER). Scout Camper, Alu-Cab, 270-degree awning, Nemo sleeping bag and pad.

Communications—Rugged GMR45 High-Power GMRS Mobile Radio hard mounted in cab with at least one handheld GMR2 for everyone in family. These Rugged Radios can also access Family Radio Service (FRS) channels. OnX app, phone, and factory vehicle GPS. WeBoost.

First Aid/Hygiene—Tourniquets, bleeding control kits, mobility trauma kits (enough for everyone in rig). Shower pouch wipes. Camping shower. Toilet paper. Soap and hand sanitizer. Trasharoo or trash carrier.

Security—.300 BLK Carbine, ammo, night vision optics, KC HiLiTES 360-degree lighting. Lockable storage and mounts. Drone. Trip alarms.

Emergency—Fire extinguisher: A, B, C rated and hard mounted. Noco battery charger, motor dependent. Innova 5610 diagnostic tool.

Recovery—Bumpers front and rear with rock sliders. Warn Zeon Synthetic Winch. Factor 55 Ultimate Recovery kit, Borah or Sawtooth. Pro Eagle jack or Hi-Lift jack. Maxtrax. ARB twin compressor and tire repair kit. Full-size spare tire. DMOS Pro Shovel.

Fire—Lighter, torch, striker, hurricane matches, starter log, wood, chainsaw.

Auxiliary—Flashlight, warning device such as flares or reflectors, phone charger, tarp, raincoat, gloves, water, basic tools, duct tape, shovel, ice scraper/snow brush. MLS from Fieldcraft. Tools and toolbox. Solar panels, Redarc BCDC, and inverter.

Civilization has a way of finding you, and eventually you're going to need the trappings of civilization to sustain life. You're going to need technology and industry to help you get outfitted with the best weapons systems for self-defense, with the best emergency equipment for fire suppression and vehicle recovery, and with the best tools for regular maintenance. The list of potential things to buy or to worry about is virtually endless if you don't know what you don't know. So, before you start making big moves that might take you down a suboptimal survival path, you have to ask yourself a lot of questions:

- Who will I have with me?

- What are my vehicle options?

- What kind of money do I have to spend on this?

- What survival skills do I have?

- Where am I going?

- Do I have an off-grid place to bed down, or am I going to live out of the rig?

- How long can I live like this?

- What are my main strengths and vulnerabilities?

- Can I live without ready access to medications?

- Do I have enough of everything I need?

- What unforeseen things am I not thinking about?

Your answers to these questions will go a long way toward telling you what kind of bug-out rig you need to build. They'll give you insight into what kind of off-grid existence someone of your temperament and ability requires. And if you're the kind of person who needs some sort of permanent footprint, who just can't move from spot to spot and live out of a camper shell indefinitely, then your answers will also point you toward what your bed-down location needs to offer you in terms of defensibility and sustainability so that you have a better chance to survive and thrive for an indefinite period of time in a world that has gone to shit.

THE MOTO BUG-OUT OPTION

Having a motorcycle as a bug-out vehicle may not be the first thing that comes to mind when people are looking for a vehicle to get themselves and their families out of a bad situation, but motorcycles are generally less expensive to purchase and easier to maintain than automobiles, and they are unmatched when it comes to maneuverability through urban areas *and* rural terrain. Building out a couple of bikes might just be the right survival solution for you and your family—as long as they're the right type of bikes, of course.

When most people think about motorcycles, they put them into two categories: street bikes, like cruisers, touring bikes, and sport bikes; and dirt bikes, like the ones you may see at the motocross track or ride off-road on the weekends. But there is another category that, in my opinion, is a better option when it comes to a bug-out bike: the dual sport and adventure class of motorcycle.

The dual sport and adventure class bikes do it all. They are the jeeps of the motorcycle world. They are designed to handle riding around in urban environments, as well as unpaved road surfaces like dirt roads, fire roads, ATV trails, and even less technical single-track trails. They are not the best at any one thing, but they can handle whatever you throw at them very well. They can also be set up to carry heavy loads—from everything you'd need on a multiday camping trip to the essentials you and your family require to relocate and make your bad situation a better one.

When searching for a bike, there are some key questions you always need to keep in mind. For instance, what are you using the bike for? Will this simply be a vehicle to get to another location where you have other vehicle options, or is this going to be your primary mode of transportation after you bug out? This might seem like an obvious set of questions, but if your bug-out bike is simply to get out of your current location and over to another place where you have resources, then your bug-out bike decision could be pretty simple: a reliable motorcycle that gets you from A to B is really all you need. Now, if this is a motorcycle that, for example, you will use to leave a heavily populated urban area and relocate to the mountains, with unimproved roads or trails, to establish a base camp, a motorcycle like a dual sport or adventure bike might make more sense.

Another issue is the load-carrying capacity. Is the subframe (rear or tail of the bike) strong enough to carry the loads you wish to pack on the bike? This includes the rider(s) *and* the gear. In a bug-out situation, being able to carry all the things you need is important. If your bike isn't designed to carry a load on the subframe, or you aren't able to attach panniers or a similar loadout system, it may not be the right bike for you. Dual sport and adventure bikes are designed to carry these loads as well as a passenger.

Beyond the weight that your bike can bear, the weight of the bike itself is a key consideration, especially if you're a beginner or a less experienced rider. You should be looking for a bike that you can ride proficiently without the weight creating doubts in your mind as to your ability to ride it. In most cases, your bike is far more capable of tackling difficult, technical terrain than you are capable of piloting, and if you feel like you are trying to wrangle too much bike in too many difficult scenarios, then guess what: you're probably right. Weight can also be a factor if the bike falls over or when the bike is on its side. If you aren't able to use the proper technique or you lack the strength to lift your loaded bike, that's a problem you either need to rectify through rider training and better personal fitness, or you need to recognize this as a deciding factor in whether you build a bug-out bike at all.

But its reliability is probably the most important consideration of all for a bug-out bike, in terms of maximizing survival capability. Some bike manufacturers are known for their reliability, while others are known for their higher performance. The trade-off for high performance machines usually means they require more maintenance to keep the bikes performing at their peak. Additionally, there is a school of thought that carbureted engines are better than fuel-injection engines, since fuel-injected bikes rely on electronics to deliver fuel, which makes them prone to needing more maintenance. On the flip side, there are some factors that make carburetors a little less reliable—elevation changes, weather changes, and fuel quality can affect how carburetors perform. You have to weigh these options and decide what is better for you and your level of experience, both as rider and mechanic. In the end, in a bug-out situation, you want your bike to be reliable and reliably fixable.

Building a reliable bug-out bike consists of few other key important factors. Many of these options are bolt-on parts that will help the bike stay running in rugged terrain by protecting both the bike and the rider. Other parts will allow you to carry the gear you need for your situation. Together, they make a legitimate moto-mobility platform.

Bike Protection Parts

Motorcycle manufacturers tend to place important components in different places. You should look at your bike and see where the vital components are that keep the bike running and protect them so that your bike stays running, and you will be less likely to find yourself stranded.

- Skid plate or engine guard—Helps protect the bottom of the engine or crankcase from rocks and logs as well as important systems such as the oil filter, oil cooler, and exhaust.

- Crash bars or radiator guards—Help protect the engine, radiators, and body parts of the bike.

- Hand guards—Barkbuster and other brands make guards that can be attached to the handlebars to protect the riders from limbs, rocks, and cold wind. They also help protect the bike's brake and clutch levers when the bike falls over.

Luggage Racks and Parts

Motorcycle luggage falls into two categories: rackless luggage and luggage that requires racks to be mounted to the bike to support the luggage. In this case we will only be talking about luggage that requires an external rack system, because external racks allow the bike to distribute the weight better as well as help with protecting the bike's rear subframe when the bike goes down.

The main calculation, and one of the trickiest things to figure out, is the balance of weight distribution, security, and physical orientation factors in deciding whether to employ hard case luggage or soft case luggage.

With hard luggage, you've got security and peace of mind, because it's usually lockable. Hard panniers can be plastic or aluminum, with most riders opting for aluminum as it can be bent back into shape in case of a drop. The three boxes can also double up as two handy chairs and a picnic table. A major downside, of course, is cost. Hard panniers are more expensive than soft luggage. Your width is also greatly increased, making filtering through traffic very difficult in urban areas. But most importantly, the top concern is that if you're actually going to ride off-road, hard panniers can break legs in a fall. Since they weigh twice what soft panniers can weigh, when you stick your foot out to try to catch yourself or you get it stuck in a rut, that heavy, hard pannier driving into your leg won't be pretty.

Soft luggage, by contrast, is cheap and easy to attach and

repair. They are also lightweight. If you're confident that whatever bug-out scenario you confront is likely to involve riding off-road, soft bags are the best choice because you can paddle through ruts and crash without the fear of your motorcycle luggage doing more damage to you than the fall itself. The only real drawback with soft luggage is security. They lack the key locks of hard panniers, though there are options on the market now that are slash proof. Still, if someone really wants to get inside your bags, then nothing will stop them, not even a lock on a pannier (which can always be smashed with a hammer and chisel). Waterproofing is another factor, but I've had "100 percent waterproof" soft bags leak less than metal boxes, so this is an issue that can always be overcome by putting your stuff in dry bags, whether you've chosen hard luggage or soft luggage.

7

HOMESTEAD

W e began this book and this preparedness journey by talking about the importance and primacy of mental resilience in survival. We're going to end it by talking about the importance of creating physical resilience within your homestead. Outfitting your homestead is critical to get right. It's where you live. It's where you raise your kids. It's your shelter. It's your security. It's where your survival is sustained and where your preparation could be the difference between thriving and just getting by . . . or not.

It's also where most people get preparedness wrong, thanks to the influence of mainstream media outlets and reality TV shows. Just think about one of the terms they use most commonly to refer to those among us who have spent time and money on modern survival skills, tools, equipment, and training to live a better, safer, more secure existence in our own homes: doomsday prepper.

They use this term derisively. When the larger population picks it up, they use it like a slur. They spit it like venom. They refuse to see any of us as conscientious or as dedicated to protecting ourselves, our families, and our communities. Instead, they insist on seeing us as paranoid and unstable, uneducated conspiracy theorists, gun nuts, and whack jobs. They see what the media wants them to see, which more often than not is angry, suspicious, middle-aged people with a house full of guns and a bunker full of freeze-dried emergency food kits with a twenty-five-year shelf life. Throw in a tinfoil hat for visual effect.

This is how many people, from novices to avowed preppers to self-styled experts, got their first exposure to preparedness, and it has affected many of their initial choices and perceptions—for the worse—whether they know it or not. Because what they were looking at when they saw those doomsday preppers for the first time were not people living high-quality prepared lives—what they saw were caricatures living closed-off, scared lives. They saw people who were the opposite of resilient, and their homes reflected that fact.

This is *not* what preparedness in the homestead should look like. The homestead should be a robustly secure yet comfortable (and comforting) physical environment with security, medical, and fuel resources to support not just self-defense and survival, but a positive quality of life for your family when catastrophe strikes and infrastructure breaks down.

FIXING THE FIRST IMPRESSION

The first impression you get from the doomsday prepper caricature is that the main reason to stockpile food, supplies, and weapons is for the end of the world. It's to defend yourself in the zombie apocalypse, to survive underground after Russia drops their nukes, to fend off violent mobs during a civil war or desperate survivors after a virus wipes out a huge chunk of humanity. And while some of these cataclysmic events are certainly possible, which means you shouldn't pretend they'll never happen (like a zombie horde), there are much more typical and obvious reasons to build up your homestead.

All we have to do is look at California and its massive wildfires, or Texas when a lot of homes had their pipes burst during a once-in-a-century freeze, or the Gulf Coast with its exposure to massive hurricanes like Ida, to find examples where home preparedness is most vital. These natural disasters and freak weather events aren't the end of the world, but they overwhelm infrastructure systems and cut off tens of thousands at a time from basic services for long enough periods that they can become life-threatening very quickly unless you have a robust, well-run homestead.

Take Hurricane Ida, for example. Thankfully, it turned out to have a smaller impact than Katrina. Though the storm had 150-mile-per-hour sustained winds (30 mph harder than Katrina), making it among the strongest hurricanes to ever hit the state, Ida didn't swamp New Orleans under a thirty-foot storm surge like Katrina did. This made Ida less immediately deadly, but only a fraction less destructive. In Louisiana, the storm did tens of billions of dollars' worth of damage, including knocking out power to the entire city of New Orleans and most of the region, leaving some residents without power for several weeks during a time of year when the average high temperature is in the mid- to high eighties and the humidity isn't much lower.*

It's what happened in the days right after the storm that is so revealing from a homestead preparedness point of view. Almost immediately, there was a secondary run on fuel at the region's gas stations. There was also a run on fuel canisters at local hardware stores and big box home improvement stores like Home Depot and Lowe's. There were multiple reports of people buying up five-gallon buckets and bringing watering cans and two-liter soda bottles to filling stations because they couldn't find fuel canisters anywhere. Some of these people were buying gas for their cars, which had already run to empty, but most were buying gas for their generators to maintain the power supply to their basic necessities.

Think about what that means for a second. A large percentage of the population along the Gulf Coast had learned their lesson from Katrina and the storms that came before it, so they smartly purchased generators as an alternate power source in case of

---

*Interestingly, during the entire Hurricane Katrina catastrophe, Bourbon Street downtown never lost power.

emergency. *And yet*, so many of them did not have enough fuel on hand, nor canisters to store fuel, to last them even a couple days. They had the means for resilience, but not the methods. They had the tools, but not the planning. As a result, there were numerous reports of fights and dangerous confrontations at gas stations and stores throughout the region, none of which could be immediately addressed or broken up by law enforcement because they were stretched thin dealing with the bigger infrastructure problems that typically arise from catastrophic events like hurricanes.

The goal of a prepared homestead is not to survive the end of days; it's to thrive every day without having to rely on infrastructure systems you don't control to deliver all or any of the services that sustain life. That this will aid you in surviving the end of days, if they come, is just the upside. This will ensure your survival and resilience every other day—good, bad, or worse. In a nutshell, your homestead should be self-sustaining for an indefinite period of time or, if you have financial and resource limitations, for as long as you can keep it going.

TACTICAL RESOURCES (SECURITY AND SELF-DEFENSE)

Security always comes first. It's how every soldier is taught, and it's a duty no soldier is exempt from fulfilling. Whether you're occupying a building for a night during an extended combat patrol or you are building out a firebase, the very first task for everyone on the team is to secure the area. And a big part of that task is evaluating and analyzing the area to determine its strengths and weaknesses so that you know where both your tactical advantages and vulnerabilities lie. Without security, nothing else can thrive. It goes hand in hand with self-reliance and independence.

In the army, there is an acronym for the system we use to interrogate the terrain and do this analysis: OCOKA.

Observation and Fields of Fire

- What, and how far into an area, can you see from particular vantage points?

- What can an enemy see of you from those areas?

- Where are the broadest, most effective fields of fire?

- Are there places with significantly limited fields of fire?

Cover and Concealment

- Is there sufficient protection from direct or indirect fire, like a wooded slope or a berm?

- Which areas offer the best and worst cover?

- Are there areas that offer sufficient concealment from the enemy so that they don't know where you are and can't see you maneuver toward them?

Obstacles

- Are there any natural impediments present, like hillsides or cliffs or rivers, that will slow down or divert the movement of forces—ours or theirs?

- Are there any man-made objects or structures, like bridges or roads or outbuildings, that can be utilized as obstructions to enemy forces?

- Which obstacles are located in advantageous or disadvantageous positions for observation, concealment, fighting, or escape?

Key Terrain

- Are there any specific locations in the area that are essential to control to maximize security or fighting advantage?

- Are there any places where we are at a distinct disadvantage?

Avenues of Approach

- If an attacking force were to converge on this location, from which directions would they come?

- Are there roads, trails, or carved paths available for approach?

- Which avenues of approach are most to least likely?

The answers to these questions very much determine how we approach securing a location out in the field. And while the tools, equipment, and methods we employ in that process are somewhat different in the military than they are in civilian life (I have yet to see a private home in the civilized world with a fence made out of HESCO barriers, for example), the questions you should ask yourself are the same. And the principles of security and self-defense that should inform how your answers affect your choices are also the same.

That is to say, you will want to exploit, manipulate, and maximize the physical advantages of your homestead and then mitigate any disadvantages or vulnerabilities by deploying a suite of technological resources designed to keep threats outside the wire and give yourself as much time and space and standoff as possible. The key considerations that should guide your decision-making here are early warning and redundancy. You want to know as soon as possible if threats are converging on your homestead or developing from within (e.g., a kitchen fire or carbon monoxide buildup), and you want to have multiple layers of observation and obstacles to aid in self-defense and escape.

Accordingly, a good security system always involves overlapping, interconnected technologies that provide abundant detection, illumination, observation, and notification. From an equipment perspective, that breaks down into three categories: sensors, cameras, and alarms.

How robust you can make that system will depend almost entirely on the physical characteristics of your living situation (apartment vs. condo vs. house; urban vs. suburban vs. rural), but the goal will always be the same: to maximize your ability to see threats coming as clearly as possible, from as far out as possible, and to know about them as soon as possible so that you can seize the advantage to fight or flee as appropriate.

MOTION SENSORS

At some level, every home security setup relies on motion detection to activate the entire cascade, from illumination to observation and notification. Working from the outside in, that starts with lights.

Motion-activated floodlights installed above points of ingress and egress, as well as pointed into spaces that are ideal for concealment, are relatively inexpensive options for maximum illumination and detection. There are a number of manufacturers who offer battery-powered setups as well as hardwired units with battery backup that are programmable, networkable, and remote controllable from your smartphone. This allows you to preset the time for different lights to come on whether you're home or away. Systems like this also let you turn on lights remotely, so when you're on your way home late at night, you don't find yourself pulling into a dark driveway.

There are obvious deterrence benefits to a well-lit property. Opportunistic intruders are less inclined to target properties where the element of surprise or the possibility for concealment has been significantly reduced, for example. Good illumination also helps to reduce self-inflicted slip, trip, and fall injuries, which make you less physically capable from a self-defense orientation, and therefore less physically resilient. There are threat elimination advantages as well, though maybe not the kind of threats you might be thinking of.

My good friend and fellow Army Special Forces veteran Tim Kennedy lives in Texas hill country and for the last few years has been waging an Elmer Fudd–level war against coyotes and snakes who keep breaking into his chicken coop in the middle of the night and killing his chickens and eating their eggs. Motion-activated lights wouldn't scare those predators away, of course, but the lights would expose them and make them clear targets for Tim.

The Million-Candlepower Flashlight

Everyone knows what a flashlight is. We all know it's important to have a flashlight in your vehicle in case you're stranded at night, and to have one in your home in case the power goes out. What many people don't know, however, is that there is one kind of flashlight that's capable of stopping an intruder in their tracks. Sometimes referred to as a million-candlepower spotlight, this large handheld flashlight produces between 70,000 and 100,000 lumens and is paralyzingly bright when pointed at another human being. Beyond its established purpose—to illuminate large areas of land or sky—it has legitimate stopping power.

Million-candlepower flashlights used to be very expensive (some high-end brands still are) and chew up batteries (some still do). Thankfully the technology has now been around long enough that there are newer versions to be found that cost less than sixty dollars and are both USB and solar rechargeable. If you live out in the country with little ambient light, it's a solid option for illumination and observation.

Inside that outer ring of exterior lights, you should also have motion sensors attached to every reasonably accessible door and window in the house. Those sensors should be wired into your home security system and, when tripped, sound an alarm and send a notification to police. You might think that is a no-brainer for home security, but you would be shocked by the number of people who forgo sensors altogether because they already have cameras and think that's sufficient, or who skimp on them because every door and window requires an individual sensor, which can start to add up.

Cost is always going to be a consideration when you're deciding how to deploy motion detection technology across your home security system, but the best solutions are not either-or propositions; they are a strategic combination of lights and sensors. Just remember: when you're thinking about the lighting element of your security system, you want to make sure you've got broad enough coverage for the purpose of deterrence and targeted coverage to reduce accident risk and vulnerability of key resources like food and water and power stores.

CAMERAS

At a minimum, you should have some kind of external camera solution for your home. For some people from older generations, I know this might feel a little odd or invasive. For most of history, security was done entirely by people you trusted. As recently as the 1980s and early 1990s, a sign that you were moving into a good, secure area was an active neighborhood watch program or a contract with a private security company that sent out a uniformed officer whose job was to drive around the neighborhood in a branded car with a roof-mounted yellow light bar to ward off the criminal element. But with the increasing ubiquity of video technology beginning in the 1990s, that began to change. Video cameras were no longer the exclusive domain of banks and government buildings and rich celebrities. More and more, normal people could afford to have their homes outfitted with cameras by companies like ADT, Brinks, SimpliSafe, or Vivint, which is the service provider I use.

Cameras quickly replaced human assets, becoming the centerpiece of most advanced home security solutions that are available to the general population at a reasonable cost. Many of those systems also deploy cameras in tandem with sensors since they support each other's functions in the areas of deterrence, coverage, and remote accessibility. A number of systems actually link them, placing small but sturdy cameras in visible locations near exterior lights that both record and alert you when the lights get triggered.

All that being said, if you live in a condo or an apartment complex, none of that may be possible. Security is the domain of the property manager or the landlord in a rental scenario, and their incentive typically is to get general coverage of the property as cheaply as possible. They're not worried about *you*, specifically. In that situation, a Ring doorbell camera might be all you can add that you can control. That's fine. Do what you can.

That's always the rule of thumb with security: do what you can. If you live in a suburban home, consider a camera array that pairs with your motion lights, ideally one that can see out to the sidewalk and across the street. You want to be able to see who's coming, not who's already there. If your setting is more rural or you have a larger piece of property, you'll want to figure out how to get coverage beyond the house itself, out to your front gate, the rear of your property, and any other spot where visibility from high ground is still obscured by terrain features (a wooded slope down to a creek, for example). If you're facing an imminent threat, and that person is trained and intelligent, there's a good likelihood those vulnerable spots are where they'll be coming from.

Where cameras go beyond motion lights from a security perspective is when you get into interior surveillance. If having external cameras feels weird, internal cameras are going to feel alien for a little while. It can seem excessive and paranoid, like *Who am I that I need cameras watching my every move? I'm not that special.* Except, you are that special—to your partner, to your kids, to your friends and neighbors. They want to be safe, and they want you to be safe, because you are an asset to your own community.

That's a good way to think about interior security: it's about asset protection. We're comfortable putting a camera in the baby's room, right? Because that child is our most precious possession. Why would we not be comfortable with cameras watching over our other prized possessions? When we consider security for the homestead, and being prepared for all types of eventualities, identifying those things (the people we love, the valuable things we can use as currency, and perishable resources that help sustain life) is a good way of identifying where cameras should be. Think of it as a nanny cam for your own personal security.

Front and back doors. Basement stairs. Garage. Kids' rooms. Food storage room. Kitchen. Gun room. These are just examples, ideas of where to start. However you decide to deploy cameras in and around your house, the thing you cannot forget to add is a multipoint technology layer for real-time observation. Whether it's an app on your smartphone, task-dedicated tablets on every floor, or a room with monitors showing the real-time video feed, you need some way to easily see what the cameras see, and you need to be able to do it portably, on the move, so you can respond to threats dynamically. You also need to think about access and Wi-Fi. Having an intermittent connection won't suffice. You need solid and stable connectivity, which is why I use satellite-based internet with a dedicated Starlink connection.

ALARMS

Nearly every modern security system includes an alarm function—either silent or ear-piercingly loud—that alerts you to an intruder or a fire and simultaneously notifies local law enforcement, fire, or EMS, usually through a dedicated landline. These systems are great. They're sensitive, reliable, fairly robust, and definitely worth having. They're also not enough, for two reasons.

First, violence in home invasion scenarios happens very quickly, so notifying police as it's beginning is already too late to be of use when it comes to actually protecting you and your family. Second, when order breaks down in a crisis and infrastructure gets overwhelmed or collapses, one of the first things that falls away is the response time on the other end of your alarm system's landline. As was the case with Hurricane Katrina and Hurricane Ida and countless other catastrophic weather events that came before them, the power went out, telephone lines went down, homes and buildings were destroyed, nerves started to fray, and immediately police, fire, and EMS were stretched to the breaking point responding to crises that were likely bigger and more urgent than any one individual homeowner's alarm system was alerting them to (if it even got through).

In either scenario, it *will* fall to you to solve your problem. As I've said before, you are always your own first response. One of the ways to be most effective in that capacity is by giving yourself more time to respond to inbound threats. An over-lapping series of alarms or signaling mechanisms (motion-activated floodlights, for example) can function as an early warning system that does just that. One of my favorite alarm functions on my current Vivint security system is an audible chirp that can be activated once the motion detection sensor is tripped. This can act as both early warning and threat mitigation by notifying me of the presence of potential invaders and alerting them to the fact that they are compromised, detected, and being watched.

Interestingly, this is an area, unlike sensors and cameras, where you're going to want to turn your attention away from technology and toward more natural and analog solutions. Toward things that don't require electricity, a cell signal, an internet connection, or any upkeep at all to function well as an alarm—intentionally or otherwise. Here are just a few examples:

FIREARMS

Firearms defense doesn't involve the same set of considerations as everyday carry or your mobility platform. Often, tacticians teach they are one and the same, but they are distinctly different because of the environmental factors in play. In self-defense, out in the world, in areas you may frequent as part of your daily routine, you may find yourself in a situation where you have unobstructed views and lines of fire toward an immediate threat. In homestead defense it's not that easy. There are some questions you need to ask to figure out what kind of setup to run at home:

- How far is your longest potential shot in self-defense? If you own acreage, that could be farther than the effective range of a pistol.

- What material is your home made of? If you have thin walls or thick walls, there are very specific ranges of muzzle velocity (fps) and types of rounds (full metal jacket vs. hollow point) you may consider.

- How is your house illuminated internally, and how is it laid out? You may want to consider flashlight and IR illuminating or night vision options. Remember, how you clear a house you don't know versus your own will produce very different behavior. Your tactical advantage could be to remain quiet and go dark, holding down your firearm, to ambush the threat or to move offensively to interdict the threat.

My preferred homestead firearm option is a Sig Sauer P320 X Legion with suppressor and Surefire white light with visible and IR laser options. Yes! I have a set of night vision goggles bedside. I know this sounds ridiculous to some, but I'm not prepared to lose, I'm staged to win. I'm looking for every possible advantage in both equipment and tactics.

The reason I've opted for a pistol for home defense is that my house is large, but I don't have an open floor plan. The longest shot I'd have inside is fifteen yards (I measured). Plus, the internal walls, like many homes, are made of drywall, which makes high-velocity rifle calibers a risky choice in terms of overpenetrating and potentially entering my children's rooms. I also use full metal jacket in 9mm because of the tight spaces and quarters. If confronted, unlike flat ranges where paper targets stand erect, chest squared, and out in the open, I may have to tactically shoot through obstacles like furniture and doors.

Make no mistake, I do have a rifle setup as well. An 11.5-inch BCM Bravo Company Manufacturing AR-15 with added magazine, a Sig suppressor, Surefire Scout Light, and LA-5 IR laser. This is set up for external threats and takes advantage of a rifle's effective range across meaningful acreage.

DOGS

There may be no better alarm system on earth than a dog. They can hear things up to four times farther away than humans.

Their sense of smell is anywhere from a thousand to ten thousand times greater than ours. They're also better at spotting movement in their peripheral vision. Certain breeds, like the German shepherds and Belgian Malinois that we use in special operations, are also incredibly smart and trainable as attack dogs. That said, you don't need your own Cujo to get the security benefit of owning a dog. A yappy Chihuahua or hyperactive Pomeranian are just as good at alerting to strange noises or people walking onto your porch.

GATES AND DOORS, STAIRS AND FLOORS

Never underestimate the value of a squeaky screen door or a heavy metal gate with a sticky latch. They might look, to the untrained eye, like regular household items in need of maintenance, but if you make a point of becoming familiar with the sound they make when they're being opened and closed, they become part of an early warning system.

The same rule applies to loose stair treads on the front porch or squeaky floorboards in the living room. They can be frustrating to live with, and the noise they make can be annoying, but they can also be an early warning that something or someone is moving around inside your home.

TERRAIN OBSTRUCTIONS AND MODIFICATIONS

Another way to produce alerts is to increase the difficulty of navigating the terrain around your home by strategically placing random obstacles between your property line and your front door. This could be as simple as having thorny bushes below the thresholds of windows and along the outskirts of porches. It could be gravel patches you install along the borders to established walking paths that are loud underfoot. In the winter, if you live in an area that gets a lot of snow that sticks, you can spray down sections with a hose so they freeze over like an ice rink, inducing loud, painful falls. You can get very creative here and utilize almost anything you have around your property to make it hard for someone to reach your front door without being heard or seen.

This is by no means an exhaustive accounting of the tactical resources at your disposal for securing and defending your homestead. Rather, it's a thirty-thousand-foot view with some targeted dive-bombs into specific means and methods to show you how the interplay between physical and technological assets can give you the most robust security solution. What that looks like for you specifically, I cannot say. It depends on budgetary constraints, the type of home you have, as well as what and how many people you are trying to protect. Answers to those questions, with a little bit of cushion built in for spending a little more than you initially wanted (as a reflection of how important security is), will put you on the path to a customized solution.

MEDICAL RESOURCES (FIRST AID, PREVENTATIVE CARE, AND HYGIENE)

In the last chapter we talked about the power of mobility assets to extend your capacity and capability for survival. That power of extension continues, and almost becomes exponential, at the homestead.

In your EDC, you have a tourniquet. You're like a medic. You can treat yourself or someone else right on site.

In your vehicle, you've got multiple tourniquets, Mylar blankets, IFAKs, and trauma bleed kits. You've become a medic with an ambulance who can treat multiple casualties on the go.

In your home, the goal is to build on those resources even further to create what would in effect be an aid station. Now you're a medic with an ambulance and a makeshift hospital where you can treat casualties more safely and thoroughly, and you can care for people for a much longer period of time.

And it's this care aspect where the power of the homestead becomes exponential. Preparedness and physical resilience aren't just about being able to pack wounds, or suture lacerations, or set broken bones. They're also about the ability to stay

healthy and get clean, to live some semblance of a regular existence while the world is going to shit around you. If a storm cuts
off access to main roads, or Amazon doesn't deliver to your location, or civil unrest has made it unsafe to travel into town for
resupply, you don't want to be in a position where subsistence is
a matter of enduring misery and austerity for some indefinite
period of time. Survival on its own is hard enough; don't make it
more difficult by slacking on the easy stuff like first aid, preventative care, and hygiene—things that can make you feel normal.

First Aid

There are two layers to first aid supplies: major trauma response and minor wound care.

We've talked a lot already about the former category, with
tourniquets, stop-the-bleed kits, splints, and things like that.
In your home, you simply need more of them. In particular, you
should have more trauma bandages, more hemostat gauze, more
packing gauze, and more medical tape. Basically, anything that
is single use should be kept in large supply.

In addition, you should have tools and supplies that support
clean work and sanitary conditions, which are essential when
dealing with large or open wounds.

Trauma shears, fabric scissors, clamps, needles and surgical
thread, saline bags and IV drips—this is essential equipment in
support of traumatic wound treatment in a sterile environment. They aren't the cheapest things in the world to buy, but

you can buy them in bulk or in individual quantities if you need to manage cost. In either case, you will find them individually wrapped so you know they're clean, and, with the exception of thread and saline, they are easy to sterilize for reuse.

Hydrogen peroxide, iodine, disinfectant wipes, rubbing alcohol—these all have multiple sterilization and treatment uses both for wounds and for equipment, they are relatively cheap, and they store very easily. You don't need all of these, of course, and not in equal or massive quantities, but you'll want at least rubbing alcohol and maybe one other because treating wounds and replacing bandages involves a lot of cleaning and sterilizing.

This probably sounds like a lot of stuff. And at the individual SKU level, maybe it is. But rest assured all of it together, even in sufficient quantities, packs and stores neatly on two to three normal shelves. The goal here is not to turn your homestead into a MASH unit; it's simply to give you the capacity and capability to function like one temporarily if the moment calls for it.

What will likely get much more use, whether in a survival situation or in the normal course of your life, are the items meant to treat minor afflictions, such as sore throats and headaches, or wounds like cuts, scrapes, and rashes. These are ointments and pills, tablets and syrups, Band-Aids and sprays—all those medicines and medical products that you have purchased on a one-off basis over the years when someone in your family gets sick or hurts themselves.

To adequately prepare your homestead, the only change you need to make to this aspect of your first aid is to buy these items in bulk. But not all of them necessarily, just the ones that are likely to get used most often.

To figure out what those things are, first you need to take an inventory of the people who live in your home or who spend meaningful time there and catalog any chronic medical conditions or regular health issues they have. Does someone have a bad back or arthritis? Does anyone suffer from migraines or bad PMS? Do you have rambunctious kids who are constantly hurting themselves? Does anyone have allergies to pet dander or pollen? Does anyone have dry skin or eczema?

If you know what those in your care are likely to need most often, you can very quickly build out your medicine cabinet into a very smartly stocked medicine closet that will serve your entire family for a long time.

Now here is the key to this strategy (and it applies to food stores, which I'll talk about shortly): you have to use these products as part of your normal everyday life. They can't just sit there in your survival shed waiting for the world to end before you consider using any of them. For one, a lot of medical products expire. They dry out or they lose their potency or they're prone to bacterial growth. But more importantly, when you segregate out things meant strictly for survival from things designed for everyday use, especially when they're the same things, it adds an unnecessary psychological weight to the survival stock.

If you're facing several weeks with obstructed roads and no power, like many of the survivors of Hurricane Ida faced, the situation is already difficult enough. You don't need to make it worse, particularly for young kids in the house, by directing everyone to the survival shed for simple things like Tylenol or Band-Aids. Instead, you want to make utilizing your bulk first aid supplies a regular part of everyone's lives on a day-to-day basis, so when things have gotten bad in the outside world, there is still some normalcy inside your homestead. Approaching first aid supply usage this way also ensures that there is sufficient turnover of the stockpile, with as little spoilage as possible.

Preventative Care and Hygiene

The biggest disservice the doomsday prepper mythology did to the survival and preparedness community was to paint a picture of unhappy, unhealthy people who were only interested in outlasting the virus, the commies, the nuclear fallout, the aliens, you name it. There's no version of the doomsday prepper in popular culture that is looking for ways to thrive in crisis. Thankfully, that has started to change with the changing face of the preparedness movement and the rise of homesteading as a lifestyle. One of the places you can see that change is in the growing emphasis on preventative care and hygiene as part of a home preparedness plan.

Preventative care involves things like vitamin and mineral

supplementation, which help your body function optimally. Dry swallowing a bunch of pills first thing in the morning can seem like a macho flex or a stupid extravagance on the surface—*Oooh, look at this guy and his prebiotics and magnesium and zinc and glucosamine and vitamins D, E, C, B6, B12, and K*—but in a high-stress crisis environment, why would you not want to be firing on all cylinders every day? To protect your loved ones and your property, it's a no-brainer.

EpiPens and Antibiotics

If you have severe allergies—to bees or peanuts, for instance—or you are otherwise immunocompromised, having a store of EpiPens and antibiotics is something you'll seriously want to consider as part of your homestead plan. Unfortunately, this is not the easiest thing to accomplish or to maintain. In the United States, both require a prescription and are doled out in moderate quantities. Neither is particularly cheap outside of insurance coverage, and both have modest shelf lives. The epinephrine in EpiPens expires after a year. Antibiotics like amoxicillin tend to lose their potency within one to two years. There are powdered versions that last two to three years, but they require you to rehydrate them with distilled water.

Start researching reliable sources for these lifesaving drugs now. Get familiar with their expiration windows and

> make the necessary budgetary calculations and compromises to be able to afford at least a modest stockpile that you can renew or replace every year.

Preventative care also includes maintaining a steady supply of devices that enhance physical capabilities and prevent degradation, sometimes at the same time. That might be orthotics to correct biomechanical problems with your feet (which could lead to injury or long-term mobility issues if not treated). It might be compression sleeves or compression bands to manage elbow or knee tendonitis. If maintaining your homestead involves a lot of physical labor, the last thing you want is to be waylaid during a critical moment when you're needed most because you can't bend your elbows or crouch at the knees.

For me, this also includes contact lenses and contact lens solution. Just like with my first aid stockpile, I buy disposable lenses and solution in bulk and cycle through them like anyone else. The only difference is that I always use the oldest in my stockpile first, and I never let it get so low that I would risk running out before the next delivery arrived. This is always how you should think about using and restocking perishable supplies: use the oldest stuff first and stack the newest at the back. It's a system you can train like any other skill, and with enough practice it will become muscle memory.

Beyond first aid and preventative care, there's hygiene. Or maybe a better way to put it is, before and beyond first aid and preventative care is *always* hygiene. Nothing fancy or complex. A good, straightforward setup for anyone can be no more complicated than unscented bar soap, hand sanitizer, baby wipes, toothbrushes and toothpaste, and maybe a set of nail clippers. A discipline many people are lazy with no matter how well or poorly things are going in the world, a personal hygiene routine that includes these few items is one of those small, daily practices that can make a big difference to survival and to quality of life.

Bathing regularly can help prevent bacterial infections and skin problems. Keeping clean makes small cuts and abrasions less likely to become inflamed or infected. Washing your hands consistently reduces the possibility of cross contamination from raw meat and vegetables during cooking. Plus, being clean just makes you feel better. Ask any Special Operations veteran what they look forward to most about returning to civilization after a long combat tour in austere environments, and washing the dust off in a hot shower is almost always in the top two.

The last piece of the hygiene puzzle is water. Because hydration is such a critical component of survival, it's very easy to overlook the need to store water or to have an available source of water for nonconsumption purposes. You can't let that happen. Whether you fill large jugs of water from your tap, collect rainwater in barrels, divert a stream into a catch basin, or buy aluminum cans of disaster water, make sure you have water on hand and that you earmark some percentage of it for washing.

The Federal Emergency Management Agency (FEMA) suggests having a two-week supply of water stored at all times. According to their guidelines that means one gallon of water per person per day, with a half gallon for drinking and the rest for food preparation and hygiene. Weirdly, that sounds like a lot to store while simultaneously being not much for cleaning, but in an emergency situation, you will learn very quickly how to wash your hands, scrub out cuts, and clean body parts with the tiniest amount of water. And in circumstances where remaining daily water resources need to be dedicated to cooking, or to the elderly and infirm, that's when you turn to hand sanitizer and baby wipes—the A and C in your hygiene PACE plan.

FUEL RESOURCES (FOOD AND POWER)

A prepped life and a resilient homestead don't make themselves, maintain themselves, or sustain themselves. They constantly need to be fueled. For you and your family that means food. For the appliances and machines that heat and cool and electrify your house, that means power. A fully prepped homestead needs multiple, independent sources of both, ideally in abundance.

Food

The type and amount of food you're able to store will depend entirely on the size and type of home you have.* I live in a normal suburban home on a decent-size plot of land that allows for a small garden and some animals. If you live in a condo or an apartment, both of those food sources are probably out of the question. As such, I'm not going to distinguish between types of living situations in this section or qualify any of these recommendations. Instead, I'm going to talk about what is possible, and you can figure out what fits into your lifestyle and what maybe you want to aspire to as you consider alternative living situations.

The Pantry

Canned, jarred, and boxed foods are a staple of survival. Canned foods, provided they are stored in a cool, dry place, have a shelf life of up to five years. Boxed and jarred foods tend to last one to two years. Dried spices, dry white rice, and ramen are about the same. These are the target date ranges to keep in mind as you stock your pantry. They are almost as important as what you stock your pantry with.

There are staples of the survival stockpile, of course. Rice,

*Water is obviously a critical fuel source for human survival, but we've talked about it enough to this point that there isn't much left to say. You need enough for everyone to drink; you need enough for cooking, cleaning, and hygiene; and you need to be able to sanitize it at scale with bleach or boiling as necessary.

beans, canned vegetables, pickled items, dried fruits and nuts, soups, jerky, granola bars. You should have as much of each of these as you can store, that you don't hate. I cannot stress this enough: build your nonperishable food store (aka your pantry) with food you like to eat! I'm Korean, and I love kimchi. You can bet your ass that my pantry will always have jars of it. Are there better choices I could make in terms of shelf life for the space that kimchi takes up in my pantry? Probably, but none of them taste as good or offer the digestive benefits, so it's not going anywhere. What is that food for you? If there is a canned or jarred version of it, don't hesitate to put it in your pantry.

The Cycle

Whether it's first aid or food, the most sustainable approach to consuming what you store, both psychologically and in terms of potency or freshness, is to cycle through it on a regular basis as part of your normal consumption patterns. Use the cough syrup at the front of the shelf. Eat the mac and cheese with the closest expiration date. Then when you go shopping to resupply your stockpile, push the old stuff forward and put the new stuff in the back. Make these things a part of your life; don't set them *apart* from it. It's the only way to survive!

I would be remiss if I did not mention freeze-dried and dehydrated emergency meals here. I kind of shit on them in the beginning of this chapter, but that was only in the context of what they have come to represent as the official food source of the doomsday prepper. The reality is that their reasonable cost and insane shelf life make emergency meals a smart thing to have. And some of them actually taste really good. My opinion is simply that you should put these at the back end of your pantry and save them for the rainiest of rainy days. They should be the E in your food PACE plan.

The Garden

If you have the space for a garden, or better yet a greenhouse, I highly recommend building one. Nothing is healthier or tastes better than fruits and vegetables you grow yourself. I'm no horticulturist, so this isn't going to be a tutorial on adding nitrogen to your soil or rotating crops to prevent fallowness. But what I can say is that growing a mix of fruits and vegetables that your family likes to eat is the best strategy.

You should also consider growing fruits that stand up well to canning and are good when made into jams. The same is true for vegetables that are good when pickled.* This will give you an annual, renewable cache of fruits and vegetables for the winter months, which can be worth its weight in gold if you live

---

*Like commercially jarred food, the shelf life of homemade pickles and canned fruits is about two years.

in a harsh climate. Eating a canned peach at the end of January, when it's three degrees and it starts getting dark at three o'clock, is like biting into a piece of summer, and it can help you get through those last brutal weeks of winter. In addition, canning and pickling your leftover produce also affords you the opportunity to trade or barter with neighbors who have other goods you might need.

Beyond the nourishment that a garden or greenhouse offers, it also offers concealment from a security and self-defense perspective, and it's a great way to give your kids some responsibility and to teach them about how the earth can provide for them if they respect it and treat it well. After all, the ultimate form of resilience and preparedness is being able to feed yourself without relying on factory farms to do it for you.

The Farm

At my house, I have chickens that give me ten to twelve eggs every day. I have two cows that give me milk every morning. I have ducks that give me fertilizer via their droppings. I have pigs that will eventually be butchered. I have dogs for security. And I have goats because they're cute and letting my young kids feed and water them is another way of giving them a little bit of responsibility and teaching them about life and death and respect for animals.

Raising your own sources of protein and fats and feeding them with the scraps from your dinner table and your garden is a virtuous cycle of sustainability, nourishment, and, more importantly, storable and tradable abundance. Milk can be turned into butter and yogurt. Eggs and flour can be turned into pasta, then dried. Eggs, flour, milk, and butter can be turned into cakes. Pigs can be broken down into bacon, chops, steaks, lard, and mince. It can be cured, smoked, dehydrated into jerky. All of these things can be eaten, stored, or bartered.

And on top of all that, these animals make one hell of an early warning system.

The Ranch and Riverland

When I think about good sources of healthy protein that can sustain my family for months, I think of elk, deer, bison, and bear. I think of salmon. Hunting and fishing are among the main ways I stay food resource independent. When I think about building a resilient food supply on my homestead, one of the most important links in that chain is what I can harvest from the land with my rifle, my bow, and my pole.

Those large game animals can yield anywhere from fifty pounds of meat (deer) to two hundred pounds (or more) of meat (bison and elk). A ten-pound sockeye salmon will net about seven pounds of filet meat. The meat from an average-size elk by itself can feed my family for a year.

Whatever combination of food sources you have at your disposal or that you can build, grow, or raise, the important thing to remember is to treat the food with respect and to consume it as a regular part of your daily life . . . because it is. The primary purpose of your food stores is not survival, it's sustenance and nourishment and growth. Self-reliance is the goal. Survival is just the ancillary benefit of having more than you needed the moment before catastrophe and crisis changed everything.

Make no mistake: this part of homesteading requires deep resolve, a desire to be a learner, and acceptance of the fact that much of your learning will be gleaned through failures, hardships, unmet expectations, humble listening, obedient hearing, and active pursuit. Still, if you commit to self-sufficiency in food production on your homestand, not only will it tie you into the rhythms of the seasons and into your community in the most advantageous of ways, but it will create irreplaceable bonds within your family—with your children especially—that will allow you all to flourish beyond your wildest dreams, both in times of plenty and times of peril.

Power

The first thing catastrophe changes for most people is their relationship to the power grid. It breaks you up and strands you, leaving you to your own devices—literally. What those devices are, how many of them you have, and how well connected they are into your home's systems are what determine how quickly (and for how long) you can bring your home back online. When you line them out, they very quickly take the shape of a PACE plan.

When the grid goes down and you lose your **P**rimary power source, the most common **A**lternate power source is some type of generator. A lot of old-school generators operate on diesel fuel, more modern ones tend to use propane, and some are hardwired into a home's electrical system and are powered by natural gas lines that are backed up with propane. Depending on its size, a generator can power an entire house or entire section of a house, but you'll want to have a system for what you decide to power up if natural gas lines are down and your liquid fuel supplies are limited. Refrigeration units for sure. HVAC systems in the winter and the summer. Beyond that, you'll want to be selective and judicious. Regardless, there will come a point when your generator runs out of fuel; and if you are cut off from resupply, then you'll have to find other sources of power.

Solar and wind technologies have become solid power source Contingencies with advances in recent years. There are compact solar panel and battery arrays for residential use currently on the market that can store anywhere from one to three kilowatt-hours of electricity, which is enough to charge major appliances for days. Similarly, there are residential wind turbine generators that tend to be less expensive than solar and battery options and have the added benefit of plugging directly into your electric system.

Both of these technologies offer ample power for essential devices in your home, whether it's refrigeration, HVAC, or internet. Their obvious limitations are that they are entirely dependent on Mother Nature to work. If the sun isn't shining or the wind isn't blowing, then recharging the battery and pumping electricity into the system isn't going to happen. Which is why these should never be more than your contingency power sources.

If your solar and wind units aren't working, then the best Emergency power source left is batteries. Battery-powered flashlights. Battery-powered generators. Inverting the battery power from your vehicles. As an array, different forms of battery power should be able to keep food cold or frozen, a few lights on, and maybe even the HVAC going (though in the winter you should think about a fire and blankets instead).

All of these options require diligent research to figure out what is possible for your living situation and what is sufficient for your power needs. Thankfully, all of that information is out there and easily discoverable. It is imperative that you do the work, just as it is imperative that you fill out your food reserves, bolster your medical supplies, and exploit the physical features of your property to secure it. For your own safety, for the protection of your family, and for the benefit of your community as a whole.

COMMUNITY IS THE FOUNDATION

Here is the blunt truth: none of the stuff we've talked about in this chapter will work nearly as well as it could if you don't have a community behind you. I mean that practically as much as I do philosophically.

If you live in a tightly knit trailer park community, for instance, now you have multiple layers of obstruction, cover and concealment, and early warning detection. No one is sneaking through the gates and around people's stuff without *somebody* noticing.

If you live on a suburban neighborhood block where everyone knows each other, now you have a full 360-degree perimeter pushed out to at least a couple hundred feet on three sides, every inch of which is defended by forward-facing homes with maximum sidewalk coverage for lights and cameras.

If you live in an apartment complex in a sketchy area and your apartment is in a bad spot, say on the ground floor backed up to an alley, but you've made friends with the older lady in the second floor corner unit, if there is ever an armed intruder on the premises, you and your neighbors can leave your apartments and maneuver up to hers, reinforcing it as a fighting position with multiple fields of fire.

In every one of these situations, you have lots of people who can provide early warning, who can provide security help, who can watch your kids, who you can barter with to round out your food stores, your ammo reserves, and your medical supplies. It's self-reliance at scale.

All of that robustness and redundancy—*all of that resilience*— is possible within a community, provided you get to know your neighbors and you work toward a common understanding around preparedness and security. These conversations can be a little awkward at first, there's no doubt about that, but they're worth the initial discomfort if, on the other side of them, you end up with a group of folks who you can call friends and who you can call on, period, when you need a helping hand.

Humans are social creatures. Who are we, *where are we,* without our friends and family, without our tribe, and without our community? We're alone, we're nowhere, that's where we are. And that is the absolute last place you want to be in a natural disaster or a man-made crisis. When things aren't working the way they're supposed to, when it starts to look more and more like every man, woman, and child for themselves—that's precisely the moment you want to have a community to lean on, to retreat to, to contribute to, and to call home.

It's your community that is going to protect you. It's your neighbors who are going to help you out. It's your local merchants, farmers, mechanics, doctors, and nurses who are going to make sure you and your family don't starve or freeze or suffer or die when you find yourself in a bad spot.

We forget that sometimes. We lose sight of the fact that "it's not what you know, it's who you know" is a real thing, and that it applies to security, sustenance, and survival just like it applies to getting ahead. And yet so many of us focus on how many followers we have on social media, while we forget the names of the family we share a fence with. How could that possibly be a good thing?

How do we expect to survive the worst day of our lives or to persist amid indefinite turmoil if we don't put in the work to cultivate and contribute to a community of people we would do anything for and who would do anything for us? We can't. There is no such thing as a truly prepared and secure homestead without the people around you who make it possible and the people closest to you who give it purpose.

Community is everything.* Remember that and you won't just survive catastrophe, you'll thrive despite it.

*In July 2020, due to rampant civil unrest and lack of adequate response from first responders, I embarked on what I believed was an obligation to give people education and tools to rely on each other. I started an online group called American Contingency. The objective was to allow people, whether in man-made or natural disasters, to have means and methods to communicate, coordinate, and depend on each other in a worst-case scenario. Although this group has been politicized in the mainstream media and by specific government agencies, there is no political agenda baked into the objectives of AMCON. At Americancontingency.com, our group has built a community that has responded to each other during both natural and man-made disasters, and been a beacon of hope for those looking for help. The way I look at it, in your community you're either a liability or an asset. Which one are you?

A FINAL NOTE
FROM THE AUTHOR

Thank you for reading this book, for taking the time. I'm living a dream and it's full of purpose because of your support. One of the reasons I started Fieldcraft Survival and American Contingency is because I missed my community—a brotherhood and culture of loyalty, integrity, and duty. It was an amazing ride with even more amazing humans, but one day without realizing it . . . it was over. As I migrated into civilian life the same feeling of belonging, of purpose, and of community was absent. That gaping hole in my heart made me sad, depressed, and long for change. So I figured the best way to bring it back was to build it myself.

The profound purpose behind preparedness isn't just the actual skill sets it gives you, but most significantly the people it connects you with. I've found that no matter your political viewpoint or your religious background, being prepared is bipartisan and nondenominational. Self-reliance, self-sufficiency, resilience, readiness—these are things we can all get behind. They're great icebreakers for building relationships, finding purpose, and investing in a thriving, prepared life.

My hope is that you read this book and you say to yourself, "Okay, this guy doesn't seem crazy." I hope that you realize, in the context of the framework and content of this book, that it's okay to apply these basic elements in your life and daily routine without feeling overwhelmed, or extreme, or crazy. Ever since I started Fieldcraft Survival, I've battled that very stigma and negative stereotype. I never wanted to be the tinfoil hat guy. I never wanted to be on the fringe. That's not who I am. I'm a freedom-loving hippie who loves my family, my goats, and my chickens, and I just want to live a life of peace and quiet for the rest of my days. My guess is most of you also want the same.

It's a simple wish, and I'm a firm believer that all the best things in life are simple. An accurate hunting rifle. A glass of Kentucky bourbon. Being kind. A Rand's cowboy hat. A Grizzly Forge blade. Radish kimchi. These things are all very simple, but what makes them so great, and so special, is that none of them are created or cultivated easily. It takes work and attention to detail to do these things right.

The same rule applies to preparedness. It's pretty simple, but it's not easy, so you have to work at it. Constantly and consistently.

That means getting comfortable with being uncomfortable to build resilience. That means drilling your fire safety PACE plan or your active shooter response plan with your kids, whether you're a parent or a teacher. That means making a point of going out once a week and working on noticing everything and everyone around you. That means going through the thought exercise of finding your threshold for the use of deadly force. That means hitting the flat range and not just getting proficient with your EDC pistol but becoming great with it. That means knowing how to bug out and when to hunker down. That means regularly testing all your equipment and being on top of the maintenance of all your tools so they don't fail you when you need them the most.

You have to be diligent. You have to train. You have to test yourself. You have to practice. Because practice makes permanent. Practice makes resilience.

I would love for you to train with me and my team at Fieldcraft Survival, but I don't really care where you train, just *that* you train. You're going to need it. The world is a crazy, unpredictable place. It's always been that way. But I would be lying if I didn't say that I think it's been particularly bad in our lifetime when it comes to events that could be labeled as catastrophes or emergencies, where the question of survival was never far away.

I do worry that the future for us is uncertain. But what I don't worry about is the solution. The thread that holds—and will always hold—the fabric of our society and our nation together is our communities. Those communities are made up of people—you, me, your neighbor—pulling together, working together, training together. How do we make change? How do we get better? How do we improve as people, as communities, as a nation? It's simple. We get back to the basics of healthy, self-sufficient living as a part of small, local communities. The sooner we realize that the solution to our problems isn't in an app designed in Silicon Valley for our smartphones built in China, or in a headline written in New York City about something happening halfway around the world involving people we'll never meet—but that it's in *us* . . . and the more resilient we will become and the better off we will be as people and as citizens of this great nation.

In the twenty-first century, we've had a major terrorist attack, two wars, more than three hundred school shootings, riots, political unrest, massive hurricanes, forest fires, tornadoes, floods, bridge collapses, supply chain collapses, recessions, and a pandemic. And that's mostly just the United States I'm talking about.

I don't say any of this to scare you. The purpose of this note and this book is not to frighten you. It's not to highlight your deficiencies or to tell you what to do.

The reason I wrote this book is to give you the mental and physical tools you need to live a prepared life. To thrive in that life. To know that you have what it takes, both literally and figuratively, to protect yourself, defend your family, and support your community in the event of catastrophe. To know that you can—no, *that you will*—survive the worst day of your life.

My one wish for you as you reach the end of this book is that, in applying its advice, insights, tools, methods, tactics, and strategies to your life, you are inspired to do everything in your power to become more self-reliant and to spend more of your precious time with your family and friends than on your phone. I want, more than anything, for you to be able to rest easy after a hard day's work. To love well and live free, not just for yourself (because you've earned it) but for the future of your children and your children's children. Trust me, they will thank you for it. And we will all be better off, not just as individuals, but as a community and as a nation, if first and foremost we are prepared for anything, come what may.

ACKNOWLEDGMENTS

I want to take the time, first of all, to thank Penguin Random House for believing in this book and journey. It took a lot of faith and courage in trying to change the preparedness narrative. Thank you to my cowriter, Nils Parker, who made my creative voice more analytical, more distilled, and composed for you to digest. Thank you to Jack Carr for being an amazing friend and writing mentor, and for writing the foreword for this book in between writing my favorite fictional series, "The Terminal List." Thanks to Shawn Ryan, a friend and former contracting buddy, for putting me on your podcast, which put me on blast. Without your trust in me, I wouldn't be where I am today. Thank you to Andy Stumpf for your friendship, laughs, and epic times spent on your *Cleared Hot Podcast*, and at your home. Thank you to Evan Hafer and all of the Black Rifle Coffee team for always supporting me, Fieldcraft Survival, and all of my endeavors. It's amazing to be a part of this journey with epic friends who love this country. Thank you to Tom Flanagan, from Eagles and Angels, for carving out an inspirational business that uses the clothing of veterans of foreign wars and makes their owners' memories immortal through something as simple as a ball cap and letting us be a part of it. Your friendship, in the worst of times, helped me more than you know. Thank you to Clay Croft and his wife, Rochelle, from Expedition Overland for their friendship, partnership, and sharing their expertise in the overland space with me. Thank you to Scott Brady and his team at *Overland Journal*—when Fieldcraft Survival was just me, he opened his doors and supported us in education and understanding best practices in overlanding. I'd also like to thank Kurt Williams of the Land Cruiser Heritage Museum for his expertise and willingness to open his doors so I could learn more about the amazing history of the Land Cruiser. I'd like to thank Alan Wang of KC HiLiTES for partnering with us and getting us the best lights in the overland space. It's been an amazing ride with the amazing people from the HiLiTES family. Thank you to Tim Kennedy, a fellow Special Forces sniper, whose friendship and experience has helped shape me greatly. Tim was the first to teach me about marketing and business. Thank you to all my trainers from law enforcement, military, and civilian backgrounds—in particular Kevin Owens and Sean Kirkwood, whose leadership and mentorship shaped me to be the man I am today. I'd like to thank Chad Robicheaux for his friendship and courage to help those in need. I'd like to thank Thom of

American Contingency for keeping an important community mission alive. Thanks to GBRS, Kagwerks, Mike Pfeiffer from LLOD, Sig Sauer, Josh Smith from Montana Knife Company, Black Diamond Covers, and all the partners, collaborators, and friends of the Fieldcraft team. A special thanks to *my* team at Fieldcraft Survival, from my executive staff that crushes it every day, to my personal assistant and her husband, who put up with my shit seven days a week, to the hardworking gals and guys that pack our orders—without you we wouldn't have a business and I wouldn't have a job. Thank you to all my friends who've been there behind the scenes breaking bread, sipping bourbon in my living room in the happiest and most difficult times. Thank you to Pearl, my dog and friend, who was there loyally by my side when it seemed all hell broke loose—chasing balls and chasing sticks. Thank you to my mom and stepfather, Mike, for being constant pillars of support through all the years of my shenanigans. Last but not least, thank you to my beautiful children and spouse, Jess, for your unwavering love and support in the best and worst of times. And finally, thanks to the responsible citizen who is prepared, courageous, and willing to fight.

NOTES

Chapter 1: The Resilient Mindset

25   **relationship between stress and performance:** Francesca Gino, "Are You Too stressed to Be Productive? Or Not Stressed Enough?," *Harvard Business Review*, April 14, 2016, https://hbr.org/2016/04/are-you-too-stressed-to-be-productive-or-not-stressed-enough.

Chapter 3: Situational Awareness

78   **is amazingly instructive:** House of Highlights, "Crazy Fan Runs on Court During Grizzlies-Timberwolves Game," YouTube, April 24, 2022, https://m.youtube.com/watch?time_continue=1&v=gxbvom9HIYU &feature=emb_title.

79   **chest level in landscape mode:** FOX 9 Minneapolis-St. Paul, "Video of animal rights protester entering Timberwolves court, getting tackled by security," YouTube, April 24, 2022, https://m.youtube.com/watch ?v=5n7q2Pazxcw.

80   **happened to be a former Marine:** 9News, "WOW! Former marine stops armed robber in Arizona gas station," YouTube, October 22, 2021, https://www.youtube.com/watch?app=desktop&v=4p5oKIDYtDE.

86 "'you won't survive'": Gemma Bath, "Tilly Smith was taught about tsunamis in her geography class. What she learnt saved 100 lives," MamaMia, August 24, 2020, https://www.mamamia.com.au/tilly-smith-tsunami /amp.

Chapter 4: Decision Point

102 "it gives you a starting point": Michael Lewis, *The Premonition: A Pandemic Story* (New York: W.W. Norton & Company, 2021), 125.

102 "is better than nothing": Michael Lewis, *The Premonition: A Pandemic Story* (New York: W.W. Norton & Company, 2021), 126.

105 protect yourself and potentially save others: Tim Larkin, *When Violence Is the Answer: Learning How to Do What It Takes When Your Life Is at Stake* (New York: Little, Brown and Company, 2017), 41–62.

105 "I have to know how to get away": Lex Fridman, "Jocko Willink: War, Leadership, and Discipline," *The Lex Fridman Podcast*, #197, July 4, 2021, https://www.youtube.com/watch?v=n2RcVEftY48.

Chapter 5: Everyday Carry (EDC)

118 nearly 1.8 million EMS calls: Howard K. Mell, Shannon N. Mumma, Brian Heistand, Brendan G. Carr, Tara Holland, and Jason Stopyra, "Emergency Medical Service Response Times in Rural, Suburban, and Urban Areas," *JAMA Surgery*, 152, no. 10 (October 2017): 983–84.

Chapter 6: Mobility

161 EPA Water Treatment Protocol with Chlorine Bleach: EPA, "Emergency Disinfection of Drinking Water," epa.gov, July 6, 2022 (last updated), https://www.epa.gov/ground-water-and-drinking-water /emergency-disinfection-drinking-water.

SCAN TO LEARN MORE

THE PREPPED LIFE